MONOGRAMS
and ANTIQUE LINENS

Phyllis Hoffman DePiano

MONOGRAMS
and ANTIQUE LINENS

For my mother, Inez Hill Norton, who instilled in me
a love of beautiful linens and fine needlework.
Thank you for teaching me to sew and embroider.

hm | books

MONOGRAMS
and ANTIQUE LINENS

hm|books

EDITOR-IN-CHIEF Phyllis DePiano
EDITORIAL DIRECTOR Cindy Cooper
CREATIVE DIRECTOR/ART Jodi Rankin Daniels
CREATIVE DIRECTOR/PHOTOGRAPHY Mac Jamieson
CONTRIBUTING WRITERS
Ann Dorer, Barbara Cockerham,
Melissa Lester, Robin Molbert
COPY EDITORS
Whitney Durrwachter, Nancy Ogburn
CONTRIBUTING STYLISTS
Kathleen Cook, Missie Neville Crawford
Mary Leigh Fitts, Yukie McLean
SENIOR PHOTOGRAPHERS
John O'Hagan, Marcy Black Simpson
PHOTOGRAPHERS
Jim Bathie, William Dickey, Stephanie Welbourne
DIGITAL IMAGING SPECIALIST Clark Densmore

hm
hoffmanmedia

CHAIRMAN OF THE BOARD/CEO Phyllis Hoffman DePiano
PRESIDENT/COO Eric W. Hoffman
PRESIDENT/CCO Brian Hart Hoffman
EXECUTIVE VICE PRESIDENT/CFO Mary P. Cummings
EXECUTIVE VICE PRESIDENT/OPERATIONS & MANUFACTURING Greg Baugh
VICE PRESIDENT/DIGITAL MEDIA Jon Adamson
VICE PRESIDENT/EDITORIAL Cindy Smith Cooper
VICE PRESIDENT/ADMINISTRATION Lynn Lee Terry

Hoffman Media
1900 International Park Drive, Suite 50
Birmingham, Alabama 35243
205-995-8860
www.hoffmanmedia.com

ISBN # 978-1-940772-27-1

Printed in China

Contents

Introduction

Plying gentle curves and sweeping lines with linen thread, women centuries ago marked treasured household linens as a means of identification and a matter of pride. Today, using similar techniques, by hand or by machine, women choose monogramming as a means of self-expression to mark clothing, bed linens, towels, and other textiles. Three letters convey one's identity in swoops and swirls.

The love of beautiful linens and finely embroidered monograms transcends centuries. From the simple cloths of modest families to the most elaborate textiles of royal households, linens usually reflected a family's status and position within society. Stories told with needle and thread present a fascinating history.

Linens beg to be stroked and simply enjoyed. The experience of folding and unfolding perfectly starched and pressed pieces still rewards those who are fortunate to collect and own them. Monograms are regarded as the crowning adornment to any precious item and represent innumerable styles of lettering and needlework techniques.

Engraving silver, gold, and other metals or engraving on paper allows us to carry our monogram to flatware, jewelry, serving trays, and stationery. A monogram not only represents a person or household, it makes a statement of style. Artisans today offer a variety of options and flair to those seeking their own mark.

The passion for beautiful antique linens and the use of monograms is explored within these pages through the historical accounts of merchants who have catalogued them, collectors who research them, and artisans who design them.

"The attractive way you set the table can also set the tone for a meal, and gently yet powerfully convey affection, warmth, and caring."

—ALEXANDRA STODDARD FROM *LIVING A BEAUTIFUL LIFE*

TIMELESS
Legacy

Defined as the art of combining two or more letters into one symbol, monogramming is a centuries-old tradition. This means of recognition—once reserved for monarchs and nobility—today has become a treasured form of personal expression accessible to all.

Magnificent handwork and heraldic symbols reveal the regal heritage of antique European linens from the bountiful collection of Robin Molbert, a renowned dealer of fine French textiles and owner of the online shop Fleur d'Andeol. In this lavishly adorned table linen, crowns placed above ornate ciphers indicate the noble rank of a marquis.

The Allure of Lace

Ethereal as a spun web, and once reserved for royalty and the clergy, lace has been prized as a treasured embellishment since the sixteenth century. Although the origin of lace is lost to history, Belgium often has been referred to as its "cradle." Today, treasures from designer Pat Kerr's personal collection offer enduring testimony to the skills of early lace makers.

TEXT BY BARBARA COCKERHAM
PHOTOGRAPHY BY MARCY BLACK SIMPSON
STYLING BY MARY LEIGH FITTS

Pat Kerr, the celebrated Memphis designer of fairy-tale wedding gowns, was a collector of lace long before it became an influence on her work. "When I was 19, I went to the Orient and was quite taken by the exquisite embroidery with fine handmade lace," she recalls. "With no forethought of building a collection, I shipped all my own clothes home in boxes and filled my suitcases with gorgeous embroideries."

As a young girl growing up in rural Tennessee, Pat was often a silent observer as her mother and her aunt worked on quilts, tatting, and embroideries to grace their homes. Quietly absorbing the techniques they employed, Pat began to understand the rhythm of the needle and the resulting lovely handiwork their hands created.

"I grew up surrounded by beautiful things in our home. My mother had very good taste, and the marvelous thing is that she taught me to appreciate really fine pieces," Pat muses.

Since the occasion of her first textile purchase, when she traveled to other countries, Pat always made a point of visiting antiques markets and street fairs in anticipation of what might await her discovery. "Lace and textiles have always been very intriguing to me, and invariably I would pick up pieces of embroidery or ceremonial robes, a collar or cuff," she notes. "I just became so fascinated with it."

After they married, Pat and her husband lived in London for twenty years. Here she found auction houses and the legendary Victoria and Albert Museum to be inspiring sources for research. Her studies of antique textiles and laces informed Pat's decisions as she viewed items at storied auction houses Sotheby's and Christie's. "The laces that came to auction from estate sales were just breathtaking, so I started making a more serious study of them," she says.

A Pat Kerr design perfect for a wedding party's flower girl or junior bridesmaid, this lace dress was crafted using insertion and patchwork laces. Handmade Milanese lace is from the eighteenth century.

"Lace and textiles have always been very intriguing to me, and invariably I would pick up pieces of embroidery or ceremonial robes, a collar or cuff. I just became so fascinated with it."

—PAT KERR

Celebrated for her design artistry with wedding gowns and couture evening wear, Pat traces the origins of her thirty-year career back to her childhood, when she often sketched designs for her own garments and delivered them to a seamstress in her hometown of Savannah. "In a small community, you don't have access to a lot of boutiques, so I started designing clothes very early," she explains.

Pat's treasury comprises historic laces in her private collection that she reserves intact, as well as a larger assortment—possibly the largest in the world—filled with pieces she uses for garment construction.

Reflecting on her lifelong love of lace, Pat says, "I was caught in the snare of the lace web through my experience with the Oriental embroideries and my mother's early teachings about respecting and protecting textiles."

ANTIQUE LINENS
and Odd Beginnings

When Robin Molbert first put down roots in France, attending the biweekly auctions at her local auction house was a favorite pastime. As the daughter of a prominent New York art and antiques dealer it also felt like home. But nothing prepared her for the discovery she made one Tuesday morning that would ultimately have her veering off on an extraordinary tangent and a new career.

"That day there was an important estate sale at the auction house and, as these things go, an impressive volume of antique furniture and bric-a-brac was on display at the morning exhibition. There were also cartons upon cartons lining the walls and filling every available niche, and in them was the accumulation of entire lives. Tucked away under a counter, I spotted four supersize bags filled to the brim with something soft—what appeared to be textiles. As the sacks were tied and knotted with drawstrings, it was impossible to know what was inside, but my curiosity was sufficiently piqued so I returned in the afternoon to bid on the lot, and as luck would have it, I was the winner!" Robin shares.

That evening she found a surprisingly elegant collection of vintage fabrics in one bag, but it was the other three bags that stole her heart. Each was filled to bursting with exquisite antique linen sheets and table linens, beautifully embroidered by hand and cleaned and folded to perfection

This was her first hands-on introduction to the world of French, hand-embroidered antique linens. As an American, an outsider, she realized very quickly that her perspective was different and perhaps valuable. Robin came from a country where so many left their traditions and cultures behind in order to start afresh, to invent, and to break new ground. But here, in France, suddenly her eyes opened to a centuries' old tradition and an art form that had been tucked away and carefully preserved between thin sheets of tissue paper in thousands of armoires, that had been passed down for centuries from grandmothers to mothers to daughters, and that had completely flown under the radar of the fine art world—and more (and perhaps because) it was an art for women.

"I knew almost immediately that I would devote myself to reviving awareness of this truly extraordinary tradition and to bringing one of the most well-developed female art forms that has ever existed back into the public eye," Robin explains. Why would anyone sleep in store-bought cotton sheets when they could have these hand-made silky and sensuous linens against their skin? Who could possibly resist adorning their bed and their dinner table with such fineries? The single most difficult thing to accomplish in business is the creation of a market where none exists. "In the back of my mind all that I could see were the delicate flowers and exquisite monograms of these embroidered masterpieces, and I couldn't help but feeling that they were the best-kept secret and had no business staying in the closet!" she says.

She built a website and opened her shop 15 years ago. In the end it was no simple feat to be heard and seen, to create awareness of an art form that had never really traveled outside of the French family, which had never garnered outside of France either the attention or the magnitude of respect that it deserved, and that certainly had never been introduced into the contemporary commercial world. On the other hand, as her mother's daughter, she had been taught from a very tender age the value of exquisite artisanship, of impeccable quality, and moreover, that what is beautiful and well made never goes out of style, at least not for very long. Robin shares, "Personally, I never dreamed that I could pioneer a business in which I would be handling such unique and glorious treasures on a daily basis and more, shepherding them back into quotidian use, but that is exactly what has happened. Welcome to Fleur d'Andeol, my beautiful little corner of the world!"

THE MARRIAGE HANKIE

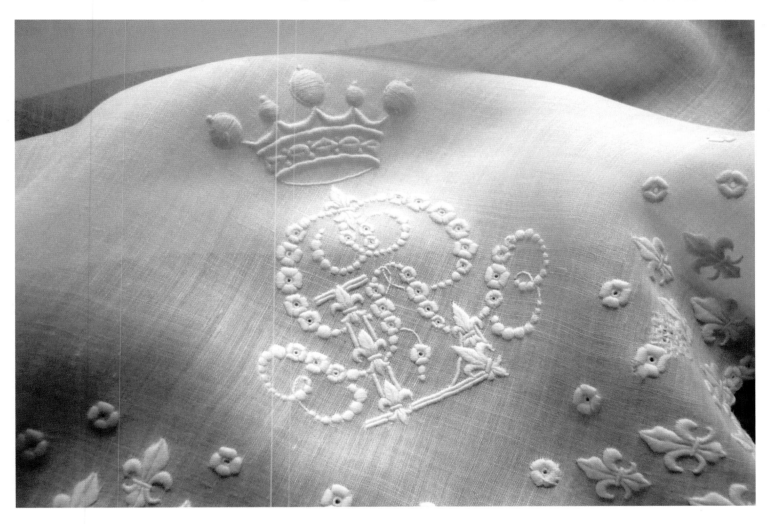

Originating in France more than two centuries ago, these exquisitely embellished
bits of cloth took pride of place in bridal trousseaus as the canvas upon which a
couple's union was proudly commemorated with elegant ciphers.

TEXT AND PHOTOGRAPHY BY ROBIN MOLBERT

So much can be said about this delicate little piece of linen that to trace the history of the marriage hankie is to drop a plumb line into the very heart and soul of France. Handkerchiefs of all shapes are known to have commonly been used by the French since the sixteenth century, but it was King Louis XIV who possessed the first collection of square hankies, initiating a trend. Later, Marie Antoinette, a fan of this variation of the accessory, shepherded it into the public eye, thus cementing it as a fashion statement. In 1785, Louis XVI went so far as to patent the royally approved shape and specific dimensions for all handkerchiefs that were to be produced in France.

However absurd it might seem that so much attention was paid to such a small and insignificant piece of cloth, it is also true that, much as bread is sometimes but a conveyance for butter or Beluga caviar, so the hankie was the humble vehicle for some of the world's most extraordinary lace and embroidery. In the mid-nineteenth century—the heyday of the French

bourgeoisie and of the production of French handmade lace—it was not uncommon for a well-to-do young woman to have six dozen beautifully adorned handkerchiefs lining her trousseau. To put some perspective on the value of these little fancies, suffice it to say that in the hundred or so years following the Renaissance, there existed lengths of highly prized lace with which a château could be purchased! It could almost be presumed that all the theatrical dabbing at tears and patting of moist brows that one reads about in the literature of the day were mere pretexts for flaunting these sublime confections.

As for wedding etiquette, what more fitting symbol of a bride's trousseau than the fairest of all—her marriage hankie? Typically made of the very finest gossamer-like lawn, marriage handkerchiefs were traditionally either embroidered around the contour, edged in lace, or both. The custom of adding the combined initials of the bride and groom debuted in the mid-nineteenth century and was highly imitated; the practice spread fast and held

tight. Often, the two letters were gracefully superimposed or interlaced, symbolizing the union of the two families and the marriage knot. No efforts were spared in creating the most intricate, original, and splendid designs for these combinations.

The appearance of marriage monograms coincided neatly with the 1859 publication of *La Mode Illustrée*, the large-format weekly French journal that chronicled, and often dictated, women's fashion. An important selling point for the magazine was the inclusion (often a double-page spread) of an elegant alphabet featuring letters designed in the latest monogram styles. The pièce de résistance was a blue-chalked tear-out stencil for marking one's own work. In an era that predated, by centuries, the invention of the television and the computer, women's social networks existed around the hearth, with journals open and needles poised. And the competition, however friendly, was fierce! On the other hand, the challenge was all inclusive; the fact that nearly every Frenchwoman learned to sew and do fine embroidery at a very tender age meant that beauty was not dictated by wealth or stature.

Because delicate marriage handkerchiefs were so highly regarded, they were often very well protected. As a result, collectors today can still find astonishing examples of these antique whimsies in mint condition.

The Royal Lineage of
TABLE LINENS

These ordinary dining accessories that grace nearly every tabletop today have become commonplace only in recent centuries, having first been introduced to the general public by a French queen.

TEXT AND PHOTOGRAPHY BY ROBIN MOLBERT

Tablecloths and napkins are largely taken for granted today—almost as much as forks and spoons. However, eating habits were not always quite so civilized, and these accoutrements have not always been the norm. There is, in fact, strong evidence that up until the late sixteenth century, neither napkins nor forks were used much (if at all) in Europe.

Fortunately, all of this began to change when Catherine de Médicis arrived in Marseille from her native Florence, soon to marry Henry II and then later to assume the French throne as queen. Catherine, legendary for her conciliatory politics and her fertile, open mind, also loved nothing more than to throw extravagant balls and sumptuous banquets. A proponent of social propriety, this well-mannered queen was responsible for introducing the napkin and the two-tined fork to the French table. Prior to the advent of the napkin, tablecloths had assumed excessive dimensions, with drops on the sides often reaching all the way to the floor. A border on the lengthwise edge of the cloth—appropriately called a longière—was, in effect, a built-in communal napkin. As depicted in numerous Renaissance paintings of banquet scenes, these ample swaths of linen came in quite handy for discreetly wiping one's fingers!

The first napkins, like the tablecloths they accompanied, were loomed of white linen damask and tended to be huge—more than 40 inches in width. They were worn tucked under one's chin to protect the precious lace collars of the period and then gracefully draped, tentlike, over one arm. A convenience whose time had most

For centuries, white linen damask has provided a fertile ground upon which textile designers could unleash their imaginations, giving rise to an extraordinary range of white-on-white motifs. Often a play on organic themes of flowers, vines, or fruit, these designs would sometimes incorporate both sacred and profane elements of public life. This page: This napkin was reserved for the celebratory feast and culmination of a hunting party.

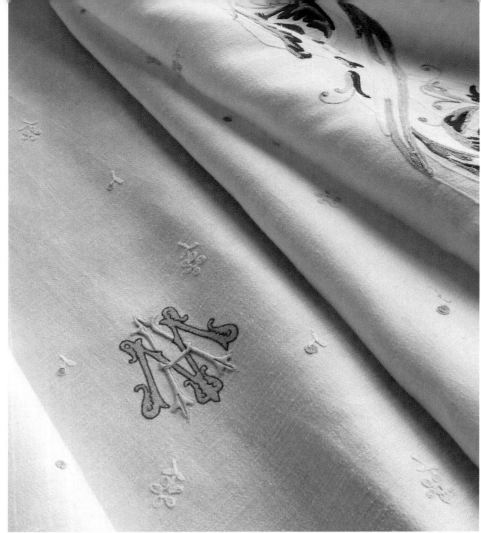

The ancient art of embroidery attained an unparalleled level of proficiency in eighteenth- and nineteenth-century France, leaving its impressive mark on period table linens. This was partly because of a steady stream of women's journals rife with the latest alphabet designs, letter combinations, and, importantly, stencils. Left: This rare tablecloth is a glorious example of the bold and unusually colorful Beauvais embroidery the Empress Eugénie made popular during the Napoleon III period of the 1850s and 1860s.

certainly arrived, the napkin almost instantly became de rigueur, and the practice of napkin pleating and folding evolved just as quickly into a new and sophisticated art form. Accomplished and whimsical design schemes abounded, many taking on the forms of animals. Sometimes, entire scenes were staged on the dinner table, replete with hunters, trees, dogs, and deer—all magically realized in the napkins' twists and folds.

It was the early eighteenth century, however, that heralded the true revolution in French dining etiquette. Much in the spirit of traditional French gardens, the dinner table became a blueprint of precise and meticulous compartmentalization. A constellation of crystal glasses, plates, and cutlery clearly designated each guest's place. Stringent rules were adopted for the orderly placement of these objects on sprawling linen damask banquet cloths, accompanied by elaborately folded napkins.

It is important to note that because, at the time, linen was labor intensive to harvest and relatively costly to produce, it was a true luxury product. And the north of France was the world capital of its manufacture. It was here, toward the end of the eighteenth and the beginning of the nineteenth centuries, that the production of these remarkable linens reached its glory. The city of Courtrai in particular (now a part of Flanders) produced the finest and most celebrated banquet cloths for nobility, as well as for anyone else in the world who could afford them.

The vast expanse of cloth provided a natural canvas for textile designers, who leapt at the opportunity to create signature patterns in the white-on-white play of the damask. Heraldic symbols were reserved strictly for the aristocracy. However, there was no scarcity of motifs for popular use: wheat ears to symbolize prosperity and abundance, bunches of grapes to ensure an excellent vintage, pomegranate flowers suggesting fertility, thistle for good fortune. Imaginations flourished, and the choices were bountiful. Wealthy families could afford to have their table linens custom designed to contain elements drawn from their personal experiences or from their heritages, such as a musical instrument; a horse-drawn carriage; a bowl piled high with luxuriant fruit; or exotic scenes representing Spanish bullfights, African safaris, or oceangoing schooners.

It wasn't until the mid-nineteenth century, however, that bold and artful monogramming burst into vogue, serving as a kind of democratizing factor in the personalization of one's linens. Whether or not a family was of noble ancestry, they did have free rein with their own initials. This coincided with the invention and mass production of the Jacquard loom—a device that enabled faster, easier, and cheaper manufacturing of damask linens. Thus, suddenly, the general populace now had the ability to purchase fine textiles, as well as to place their own individual stamp on tablecloths, napkins, towels, and sheets. This tradition enjoyed a surge in popularity that, for the next 150 or more years until the present, continues to endure. Today, one can't help but marvel when witnessing the infinite variety of alphabet styles; the sinuous complexity of letter combinations; and the extraordinary time, effort, and talent that went into these signatures. This centuries-old needlecraft has the power to transform an item as domestic and quotidian as a tablecloth into a personal work of art.

The Mark of
NOBILITY

Once the adornments only of royalty and the upper echelons of French society, monograms, with their enduring beauty, have become an egalitarian art form in modern times.

TEXT AND PHOTOGRAPHY BY ROBIN MOLBERT

Whether an impression left on the red sealing wax of a royal edict, the concrete footprints in front of Grauman's Chinese Theatre, or even the inflated bubble letters that wallpaper trains, overpasses, and tunnels in the form of modern-day graffiti, humans have for centuries yearned to leave a personal mark in the sands of time. In fact, some of the very first recorded monograms date back to the ancient Greeks, who etched walls and pottery vessels with grapheion—the classical Greek term for written letters.

During the Middle Ages in Europe, before the printing press would democratize reading and writing, most adults, including many kings, queens, and overlords, were illiterate. The royal courts, however, were generally populated with those who could read and write, as well as render elegantly. Thus, it was at this time that the art of heraldry blossomed. All manner of decrees and formal documents were stamped with magnificently designed seals, only to be signed with an inked thumbprint or a single scrawled letter—the earliest monograms.

Families with noble lineage have long incorporated heraldic symbols into ornamental design. Opposite: This napkin, part of a commemorative table service created for Louis XV, celebrates his reign in the storied weave of the damask. This page, top left: The mirror-image *RR* monogram and baronial crown is likely one of a suite of the Rothschild family's signatures.

At the time of the Renaissance, just as the printed word enjoyed its debut, so followed the embroidered word, as it was then that the sampler was born. Young girls throughout Europe participated in the creation of cross-stitched works of alphabets, numbers, and symbolic images as they practiced their hand at the embroidery that would later serve to mark and embellish their household linens. Although the formal education of girls would not be encouraged for centuries to come, and perhaps even because of this fact, women took it upon themselves to develop and perfect the art of the home.

As early as the year 1586, the French publication La Clé des Champs (The Key of the Fields), one of the first of many such pamphlets featuring stylized animal and floral patterns, would inspire this growing coterie of young female embroiderers. If one were to combine the very human desire for self-immortalization with the unquenchable thirst for beauty, one result might very well resemble the encyclopedic wealth of ornamental ciphers, monograms, and symbols that proliferated over the next several hundred years. In the Dictionnaire Encyclopédique des Marques & Monogrammes (Dictionary of Marks and Monograms) alone, an impressive work compiled by Oscar-Edmond Riz-Paquot and published in France in 1892, there are 12,156 illustrations!

These decorative elements were, in large part, initially created and reserved for the aristocracy, with the goal of producing personal, iconic images that by virtue of their singular beauty and symbolic strength imparted a sense of power while remaining easy to recognize. Very often, animals figured prominently in these renderings. John, the Duke of Berry, chose for himself the swan and the bear, while Napoléon Bonaparte selected the bumblebee. Whether a crest, a coat of arms, or a simple motto, these emblems were reproduced on each noble household's personal silverware, porcelain, linens, and sometimes even furniture, such as marriage chests and armoires.

When it came to royal and other nobly destined table linens, the signature motifs were first incorporated into exquisite designs in the damask weave. Embroidery was limited to the discreet and purely functional cross-stitched initials that appeared on one corner of the piece to serve as identification. Sometimes these were accompanied by a number, as table linens such as napkins were produced in abundant quantities and thus needed to be rotated to assure equal use. Articles of lingerie, layettes, and bed linens were also embroidered on the body of the piece with a small crown or other figure stitched in raised whitework to indicate the status of the owner.

It wasn't, however, until the post-revolutionary period of the nineteenth century that much more elaborate and lavishly embroidered monograms became a key adornment on household linens. It was here that the symbol of one's patrician heritage would be incorporated. No matter that the French monarchy had been rigorously opposed and overthrown; clearly, its attraction remained as compelling as ever! Thus, nineteenth-century France experienced not only the rise of an important bourgeois class, but with it the elevation of the signs of highborn lineage to a popular and revered art form. Whether the soberly braided band indicating the station of a baron or the much more decorous crown of a marquis, these familial symbols were embroidered with dexterity and spectacular precision on everything from babies' diaper covers to the most prized of ceremonial family linens, marriage and birthing sheets.

The increasingly rare examples of linens bearing signs of noble provenance that can be found intact today embody a slice of both the public history of France and a more private history of Frenchwomen's passion to embellish their homes. As such, these remarkable textiles remain highly appreciated and avidly collected. Their timeless beauty continues to inspire, and their endurance is a testament to the inimitable quality of this ancient craft.

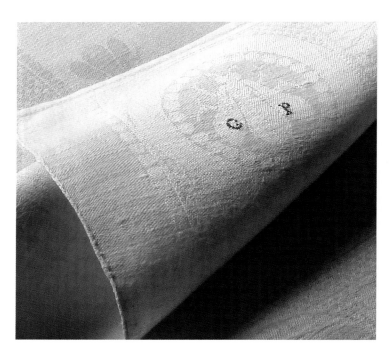 

Embroidery on household linens was initially reserved to letters discreetly marked in a corner for identification purposes. Above left: This important linen damask napkin, with its signature bumblebee motif, dates from circa 1800 and was included among the imperial linens at the court of Napoléon Bonaparte. By the mid-nineteenth century, embroidered monograms had become so popular that they appeared on everything from the most coveted ceremonial table and bed linens to everyday kitchen towels. Above right: A baby's diaper cover from the turn of the twentieth century is embroidered with the word Bébé and a tiny crown.

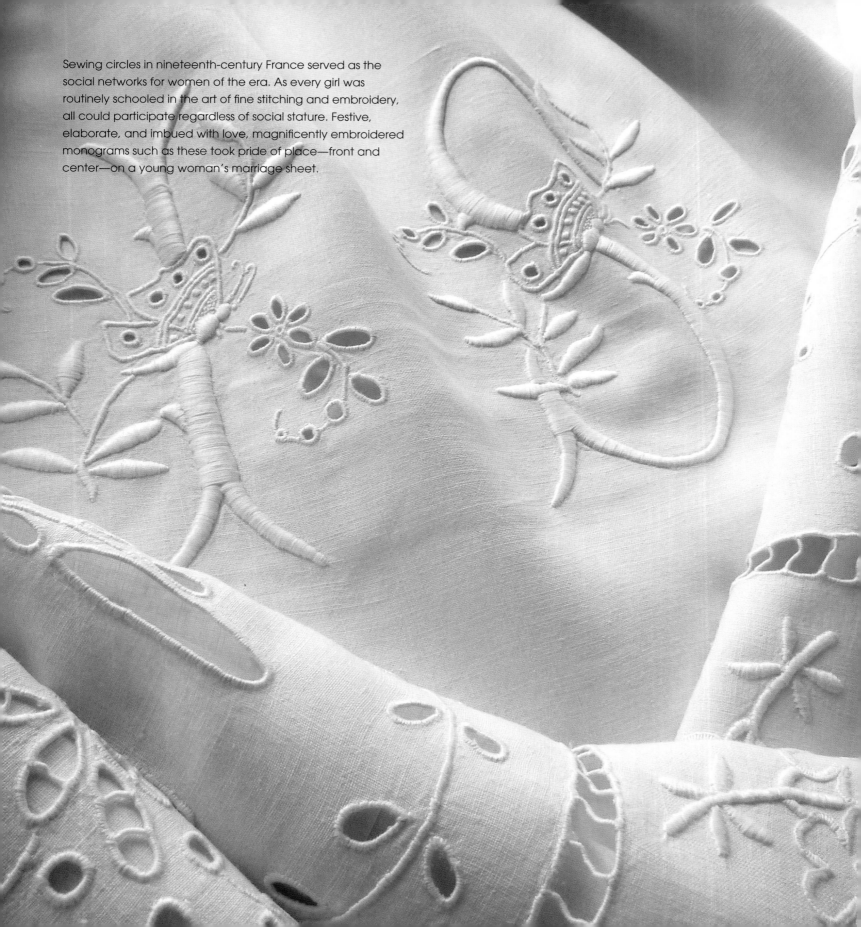

Sewing circles in nineteenth-century France served as the social networks for women of the era. As every girl was routinely schooled in the art of fine stitching and embroidery, all could participate regardless of social stature. Festive, elaborate, and imbued with love, magnificently embroidered monograms such as these took pride of place—front and center—on a young woman's marriage sheet.

The Trousseau:
A WORK OF ART AND LOVE

The romantic tradition of young girls compiling a cache of handmade finery and household goods
in preparation for their future betrothals has been part of the marriage ritual for centuries.

TEXT AND PHOTOGRAPHY BY ROBIN MOLBERT

The trousseau, or dowry, can be traced all the way back to the Roman Empire. It was the bride's counterpart to the *propter nuptias*, which in Roman law was the donation required of the groom's family to ensure a solid foundation for the newly married couple. It could include money, livestock, real estate, furniture, and basically anything else of value they could afford to give. In turn, the bride arrived with a *dot*—her family's offering of household linens, clothing, and other valuables.

The French word *trousseau* derives from the verb trousser, which means "to wrap up in a package." The size of this marital parcel was generally commensurate with the wealth of the family. Interestingly, the Christmas stocking has its origins here as well. According to legend, Saint Nicholas tossed gold coins into the stockings of the poorest young women in the village. In doing so, he granted them a dowry that, in turn, made them

Rooted in the French verb trousser, meaning "to wrap up in a package," the trousseau was literally the "marriage parcel," and a heavy one at that, as it contained all the linens a family would ever need. This page: This lovely sheet, appropriately feminine and delicate, served as a drap d'accouchée—the ceremonial half-sheet that was spread over a new mother's bed, enabling her to receive visitors and to introduce her newborn child with elegance and style.

eligible for marriage. For aristocratic families, dowries were legends of another kind entirely. One notable example was the "bridal package" of the Portuguese Princess Catherine of Braganza. In 1661, upon her marriage to King Charles II, the entire cities of Bombay and Tangier were offered, among other things, as part of her trousseau.

For French families in general, regardless of economic status, this cache consisted largely of beloved linens. Certain among these were already heirlooms, given that household linens occupied a significant portion of a family's wealth at this time. As such, these textiles were carefully preserved and passed from mother to daughter throughout generations. Most items, however, were newly created and embellished by the bride-to-be, who spent many years of her adolescence and young adulthood sewing and embroidering in anticipation of her life as a married woman. Because the trousseau represented all the linens a woman's future family would ever need, the marriage basket was a heavy one. Typically, it contained multiple dozens of dish towels, hand towels, nightgowns, petticoats, and handkerchiefs, in addition to more elaborately embroidered ceremonial tablecloths and bedding.

True to the word, it was a labor of love. And nowhere was this more manifest than in the realization of each young woman's marriage sheet. The expanse of pristine white fabric provided the blank page for her creative imagination, and, together with the marriage hankie, was the expression of her most accomplished handiwork. Embroidered with flowers and bows, threaded with ribbons, and edged in lace, these spectacular and romantic treasures sometimes required not only months but years of patient and devoted stitching. Although impossible by today's standards to measure such a task in monetary terms, what is undeniable and continues to emanate from these stunning works of art is the love that brought them into being.

The Fine Art of Fine Linens

TEXT AND PHOTOGRAPHY BY ROBIN MOLBERT

Linen, that most noble of textiles, is one of the earliest products known to civilization as well as the earliest vegetable fabric to have ever been woven. Remnants of its long and illustrious history have been recovered perfectly intact from the tombs of Egyptian dignitaries and kings. A remarkably durable textile due to its unusually long and sturdy fibers, linen is also stain resistant, hydrophobic (quick drying), very healthy as it's hypoallergenic, a fabric that breathes, keeping us warm in winter and cool in summer, and not to mention beautiful and deliciously crisp and silken against the skin. Not surprisingly, given this "laundry list" of exceptional properties, it has maintained its superior status as a luxury product throughout the centuries; and Northern France (parts of which are now Belgium) became, due to a convergence of particularly favorable geographical and climactic conditions, the world capital of luxury linen production.

As linens were not only an integral part of every French home but also a major French luxury industry, the assorted linens of the trousseau represented the actual wealth of many families, and thus the fine adornment of these items—especially the marriage sheet—took on great significance for every French

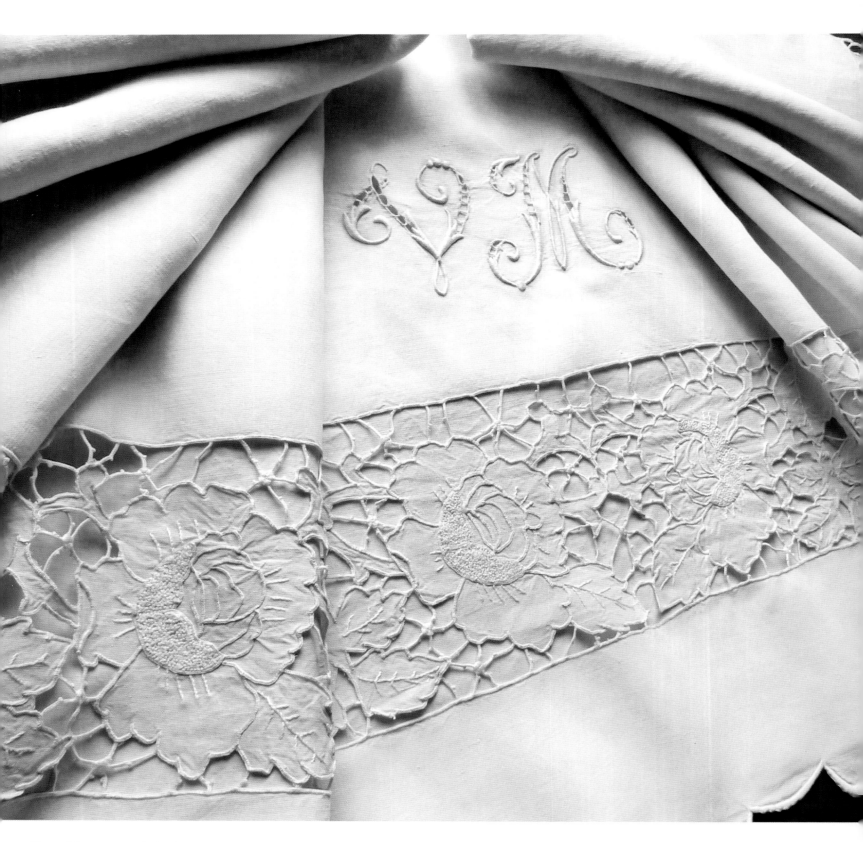

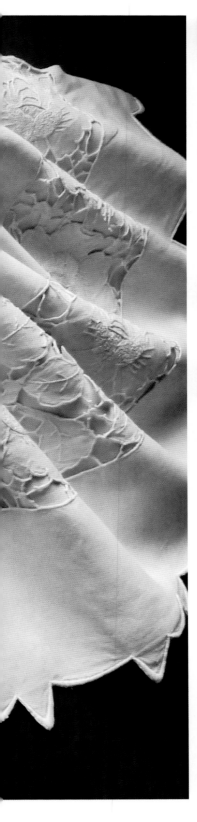

female. The family's "story" was often incorporated in embroidered symbols, be it the elaborate monogramming of the couple's intertwined initials, crowns and coats of arms indicating the family's social status, or the endless array of floral and vegetal motifs that referenced elements of their heritage and lifestyle— wheat ears and grape vines representing the harvest, pomegranate flowers symbolizing fertility and abundance, the fleur de lys marking noble descent, and much more.

Every girl's apprenticeship in the fine arts of embroidery and lace making began in childhood with samplers and embroidery exercises, and girls from every station of life participated whether they were the daughters of humble farmers or those of chatelaines and queens. It was a rigorous and exacting training that would last all of her life, but as it was also one that she shared with every other French woman, sewing and embroidery circles grew to be one of the most important female social networks of the seventeenth, eighteenth, and nineteenth centuries in France. Women's journals, publishing the latest de rigeur designs, grew in number and popularity, and whole industries bloomed around the making of stencils and marking tools. As such there was both widespread sharing of techniques and patterns as well as fierce competition to produce the most elaborate and beautiful works of art on these linen "canvases."

This female phenomenon that took France by storm for approximately 300 years has given us a window into one of the most highly developed and exclusively feminine art forms the world has ever known; fortunately it has left a good number of its masterpieces fully intact at which we still can marvel.

The Allure
of Luxurious Linens

Evocative of the eclectic architecture in Europe, the home of designer Beth Claybourn
showcases objets d'art curated during frequent trips abroad. Among these treasured
finds, exquisite textiles offer a nod to her Southern heritage.

TEXT BY MELISSA LESTER
PHOTOGRAPHY BY MARCY BLACK SIMPSON

ultivating beautiful spaces comes so instinctively to Beth Claybourn that the Louisiana-based interior designer could never imagine following a different career path. "You give a lot of yourself to clients," she says of the forty years she has dedicated to transforming American residences. "But I can always look back and say, 'This has been such a rewarding day.'"

Beth endeavors to highlight each family's style while leaving no trace of her own preferences. But Ma Maison—the Baton Rouge manor she shares with her husband, Garrett—bears the entrepreneur's imprint throughout. Natural stone imported from Europe gives a sense of timelessness, and resplendent furnishings reveal the couple's affinity for French antiques.

Amid wooden pieces adorned with intricate carvings, inlays, or ormolu, whisper-soft linens serve as delicate counterpoints. Beth christened one of her guest rooms the Napoleon Room, a tribute to Empress Joséphine de Beauharnais's regal Château de Malmaison, near Paris. The other she fondly calls the Moffett Suite, in honor of friends who visit frequently. Both boudoirs feature sumptuous layers of hand-embellished alabaster bedding. Overnight guests often descend the staircase in the morning declaring they feel as though they have spent the night in a luxury hotel, Beth says.

Although world travel influences the look of these quarters, the journey that inspires their ambience is one of sentiment. Beth's lilting drawl reflects the gentility of her upbringing in Mississippi. She recalls the childhood pleasure of slipping into breathable cotton sheets her mother had lovingly monogramed and hemstitched. She also starched the pillowcases so that the fabric would not crease her daughter's face—a thoughtful gesture that left a distinct impression.

Today, the designer advocates reserving a significant portion of any remodeling budget for planning a romantic haven. "When you carry yourself to that bedroom, it needs to be tranquil," she maintains.

In the Napoleon Room, an ethereal linen-chiffon throw balances elaborate details on an assortment of pillowcases edged with handmade lace.

An exuberant hostess, Beth often orchestrates grand soirées with live music and celebrity chefs. "Around here, everything rolls up at 11 o'clock," she quips, noting that this prompts many people to organize dinner parties. "If guests sit down together at the table, they want to linger," she adds.

White or ecru linens are a must for formal entertaining, says Beth. Against the elegance of this neutral backdrop, she builds interest with colorful china, lush bouquets, and a mélange of heirloom silver.

Passionate in her belief that gracious elements enhance one's surroundings, she often presents a set of embroidered napkins to clients at the close of a project. "Homeowners strive for comfort," she explains, pointing out that today's easy-care textiles can be as practical as they are lovely. "There is beauty in simplicity."

Sparkling
BILTMORE
INSIGNIAS

Rising from North Carolina's Blue Ridge Mountains, this stately American castle stands as a testament to the vision of George Washington Vanderbilt, who built a family home—and a prestigious legacy—that has endured for generations.

Constructed at the height of the Gilded Age, Biltmore estate represents one of the greatest undertakings in the history of American architecture. George W. Vanderbilt, the third son of railroad magnate William Henry Vanderbilt, visited North Carolina frequently with his mother during the 1880s. Smitten with Asheville's majestic scenery and temperate climate, the wealthy heir purchased 125,000 acres and commissioned famed New York City architect Richard Morris Hunt to build a "little mountain escape."

Hunt designed the opulent summer home in the style of working estates in Europe. Inspired by France's Les Châteaux de la Loire, Biltmore is the largest private residence in the United States. The sprawling 4-acre, 250-room mansion took more than six years to complete. Both the interior and the exterior bear the fingerprints of George and his wife, Edith Stuyvesant Dresser. The couple's refinement, gained through international travel, educational pursuits, and cultural enrichment, is reflected in the opulence of the residence.

In affluent society of the day, it was customary to have items personalized. George and Edith embraced this tradition wholeheartedly, adding their monogram to china, crystal, silverware, serving pieces, tablecloths, napkins, toiletries, and bedding. Even the servants' livery bore the familial mark.

Biltmore's official monogram is an ornate cipher with George's initials layered in elaborate script. These letters figured prominently in items used in entertaining, as well as in day-to-day life. The exterior of the château features a more stalwart V accented with acorns—the insignia repeated throughout the structural elements of stone and copper.

The property also houses artifacts monogrammed for George's wife, parents, and daughter. Edith's monogram was a simple EV, while daughter Cornelia Stuyvesant Vanderbilt's emblem was derived from George's signature cipher.

Above: The château's exterior pays tribute to the Vanderbilt name, with the initial V featured prominently along the roofline. Acorns, a favored family symbol, further distinguish the fabrication.

One of the most noted items on the estate to be adorned was a 1913 Stevens-Duryea C-Six. According to local legend, when the new automobile arrived, Edith found the original dark color a dismal choice. She ordered the car repainted a cheerier off-white with black pinstripes and added a feminine touch by requesting her initials be added on the rear doors. In a culture that viewed success and social rank through a monogrammed lens, the Vanderbilts reigned in a class all their own.

More than a century after its construction, Biltmore stands as a monument to American prosperity and ingenuity. With its splendid spires stretching toward the heavens, George and Edith's family home has been engraved in history.

Dining was a formal affair during the Gilded Age, with customized china, crystal, linens, and silver heightening the luxurious ambience. Cornelia Stuyvesant Vanderbilt's monogrammed china could be used interchangeably with her father's.

Linens *for* Everyday Enjoyment

Martha Lauren displays delicately embroidered linens throughout her house. The pleasure she derives from finding a dainty, intricate piece is immeasurable. Linens should be used in our homes and enjoyed as vintage linens that have withstood the test of time.

Finding one's monogram on a vintage cloth is exciting. Many collectors stick to their own initials in various designs and colors, while others collect fine examples of beautifully plied stitches.

Vintage linens, especially the hand-embroidered cloths, should be displayed as a part of your décor. Linens live when they are used and laundered rather than being stored away. Why not use them every day? A carefully placed cloth adds richness to the room.

White-on-white embroideries are elegant. The elegant cutwork designs are intriguing and take hours to complete. The embroideress actually cuts away the fabric when the stitching is completed, leaving the stitches suspended in the cloth. Cutwork allows light to come through the stitches.

Another technique that is prevalent in older embroideries is pulled threads. This technique gives a similar look to cutwork, but the fabric is not cut from behind the stitches. The threads actually pull the fibers of the cloth creating "holes" in the pattern, like the one shown above. The square in the center of the cloth is pulled work.

In surface embroidery, stitches are actually on top of the fabric surface. While the needle passes through the cloth, the embroidery design sits on top of the fabric surface. The pillow shown at the left has a wreath stitched in satin stitch creating a raised texture.

On the opposite page, the cloth with the initials LTB is hand embroidered in a padded satin stitch. When the embroideress stitched this lovely monogram, stitches were placed on the fabric to create a pad. Then in the final stitching of the monogram letters, satin stitches were placed over the pad giving great dimension to the letters. The extra steps of putting preparation padded stitches first gives the monogram a deep dimension where the white-on-white letters show very nicely.

Lacework is very tedious, and for the embroiderer it took time and attention to minute detail. Finding a pristine piece of lacework is truly a treasure. Lace, with its more delicate fibers, can deteriorate in time. A grouping of finely embroidered pillows is the perfect way to display your collection. Just as these items were used daily by their maker, you too should enjoy them every day. Avoid using them in high-traffic areas where they will be handled often.

When shopping for embroideries and laces, the sturdiness of the fibers and fabrics needs to be taken into account. If stitches are tattered and lace is torn, pay close attention to the durability. If you are not going to use the items, but are purchasing for the needlework examples, then carefully store your items.

Beautiful lace and linens will bring beauty to your home. The love of beautifully plied stitches and intricate lace is enjoyed by many collectors. When you are fortunate enough to find a lovely piece, carefully launder it by hand. Treat your embroideries and lace gently, and they will last for years.

Wrought BY HAND

What began centuries ago as a utilitarian practice—marking the corners of family textiles to identify them when laundering was a communal activity—has evolved into a beloved tradition of embroidered monograms.

Soft as new-fallen snow, wispy white antique linen handkerchiefs from CaroLinens are embellished with artful handwork and letters that exhibit the timeless grace of bygone days, when every intricate stitch of a lady's whitework revealed her genteel nature and creative ability. Artistic personalization elevates common linens beyond their practical use and transforms them into treasured pieces to be preserved, displayed, and passed on to future generations.

Feminine flowers pirouette across the corners of a Victorian-era Ayrshire-embroidered handkerchief. Trailing vines, delicate leaves, and decorative flourishes come together in an enchanting dance of stitches to spotlight a monogram. Whitework characterized by floral designs of firmly padded satin stitch and fine needle lace, Ayrshire embroidery blossomed in nineteenth-century Scotland. Collectors prize these eye-catching examples of exceptional needlework.

LINEN DREAMS

A retired teacher finds bliss discovering vintage linens,
restoring them to their former glory, and placing them
in the hands of appreciative customers who will use
the lovely items for years to come.

When Carolyn Gallier, of Mechanicsville, Virginia, stepped out of the classroom in search of a new future, little did she know she would find her greatest joy by peering into the past. "I walked into a recently opened antiques mall," the retired schoolteacher remembers. "My heart started racing, and my palms started sweating. I knew this was it—this was what I needed to be doing."

Carolyn had dabbled at selling antiques during her teaching days, but while standing in that mall, her new career path became evident. "I wasn't sure exactly how I would do it," she says with a laugh, "but I knew something old was calling my name."

A matelassé baby quilt discovered during a day of antiquing with a friend inspired her passion for vintage linens. Long discarded, the white-on-white quilt with a teddy bear in the center lay crumpled in a heap. The dealer was asking only $10 for the blanket, but when Carolyn held it up and realized its noticeably less-than-pristine condition, her friend urged her to pass it by.

Undaunted by its shabby state, Carolyn bought the quilt. While restoring the forgotten heirloom, she realized she had found her niche. "I couldn't refinish furniture," she admits, "but I could refinish linens. At one point this quilt was beautiful, but someone let it go. I knew I could bring it back."

So began Carolyn's quest to find and refurbish old textiles. In the antiques business for twenty years now, she has a new venture—an online vintage-linen shop called CaroLinens. Although she is reluctant to be identified as an expert (she instead refers to herself as a "lover of linens"), her keen eye for treasure hunting, her skilled hand at restoration, and scores of her repeat clientele attest otherwise.

The entrepreneur sells her merchandise at varying price points because she wants every customer to come away with something that will make her feel good, add beauty to her home, and provide years of practical use. "My biggest pleasure is finding things I know people will love and use," Carolyn says. "That's my purpose."

Madeira-embroidered handkerchiefs are ornate yet suitable for everyday use.

Whispers of *Timeless Traditions*

Bridging the past and the future, the owner of this Williamsburg, Virginia, antiques shop utilizes her expert knowledge of textile history and her talent for revitalizing late nineteenth- and early twentieth-century linens for customers to use and enjoy today.

I've often said, 'If the linen could speak, it would tell us where it was made, who spun it, and in what mill in Ireland it was produced,' " says Sandy Patterson, proprietress of High Cotton, Ltd., in Colonial Williamsburg, Virginia. "Since it can't talk, we look for the clues."

Sandy fills her shop with fine estate linens, crystal, silver, china, and glassware dating from 1880 to 1940. As visitors enter the store, they often sigh with appreciation as they take in the nostalgic ambience. Bedroom and living-room vignettes throughout the 2,000-square-foot space invite guests to linger. "A lot of customers say, 'This reminds me of my grandmother's home,' " she adds.

In a city known for antiques, High Cotton is a must-stop destination for textile lovers. With a practiced eye, Sandy unravels threads of history as she inspects her inventory. Evaluating the quality of the linen and noting how it was made offer indications about the piece's origin. The style of embroidery—even the size of the monogram—helps reveal an item's provenance.

A rare collection of silver napkin clips, circa 1910 to 1930, readies a bundle of hemstitched napkins for service. Monogrammed clips provided a helpful means of identification when napkins were not laundered after every meal.

Continental girls in the 1800s began their apprenticeships in sewing and embroidery at age 6. Proficient by 14, a young lady would start preparing her trousseau, stitching her own initials on household linens but leaving space for her future husband's—his identity a distant, dreamy mystery. Although needle arts eventually faded from standard feminine education, the tradition of collecting bridal accoutrements continued for decades.

With more than twenty years in the business, Sandy says her greatest satisfaction comes not in uncovering the history of antiques but in giving them a future. "My favorite part of the job," she shares, "is finding linen that has been stored away for forty or fifty years and restoring it to its original beauty."

Monogrammed selections are perennially popular, with half of the shop's customers seeking their own initials. The other half are more concerned with the artfulness of the work than with the specific letters embroidered. "They are all enthralled with the quality of the handwork," the entrepreneur points out.

High Cotton specializes in the care and storage of these delicate items and even offers a European laundry and pressing service on the premises. Sandy also conducts in-store presentations on the history and restoration of vintage linen and lace.

With so many exquisite linens available, collectors could make purchasing decisions based on a complex rubric that considers the fabric origin, fiber quality, embroidery techniques, and age of the piece. But ultimately, Sandy says, for most High Cotton patrons, the motivation is generally more personal: "In the end, they buy whatever pulls at their heartstrings."

VINTAGE
Embellishments

The timeless allure of white-on-white décor drapes a home in unmistakable elegance. Whether crisp and clean lined for a polished look or softly kissed with adornments for romantic style, white gives interiors a sense of calm. Because monograms add character to household linens, everyday objects make every day beautiful.

Household linens for married couples may be embroidered in a variety of ways. A single initial representing their surname is always a classic choice, but various two- and three-letter versions offer options for displaying their owners' unique style. Opposite: A ribbon-wrapped bundle of blossoms brings a touch of spring to this monogrammed tablecloth. Above: A breezy white top sheet is folded to expose the first initials of husband and wife.

A single initial adorns this vintage handkerchief. Opposite: Freshly pressed, this hemstitched sheet with a stately cipher is ready to dress tailored bed furnishings.

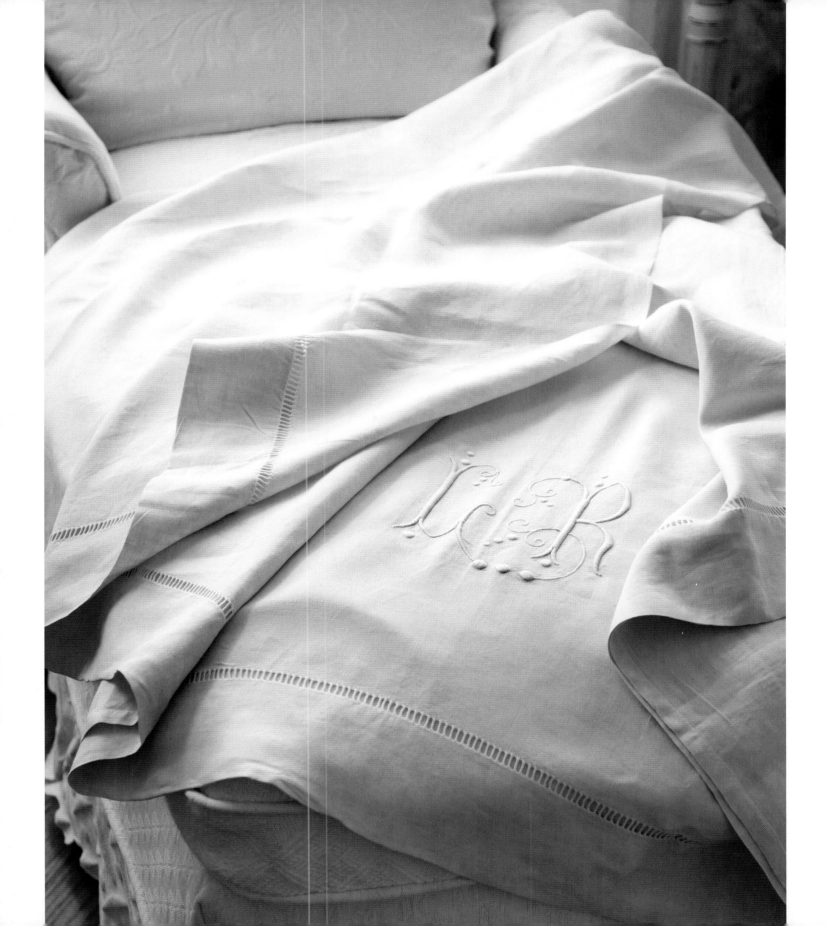

While combing estate sales, antiques dealer Carolyn Gallier of CaroLinens often unearths drawers full of linens that have been hidden away for years. "The older generations saved things," she explains. "They used them for special occasions. But at some point, they could be packed away and forgotten." Carolyn encourages her customers to live with their linens, pointing out, "Linens do better if people use them." If well cared for, heirloom fabrics can offer years of enjoyment and practical use.

EUROPEAN LINENS

"To love beautiful linen," wrote French novelist Louise de Vilmorin, "is to love fair weather, fair weather . . . that one can acquire and carry home."

TEXT BY ANN T. DORER
PHOTOGRAPHY BY JIM BATHIE
STYLING BY YUKIE MCLEAN

Delicate designs on damask linen are said to play hide-and-seek with the light. The scalloped edges of these linens are further enhanced by a fringe that begins like lattice work and ends in long, fluffy strands.

Throughout the ages, fine linens have been cherished and valued as much as silver and fine porcelain. To gently run your fingertips over the soft sheen of antique linen fabric is to personally touch the past. Getting the trademark luxuriously soft feel European linens are known for all begins with a flax plant. Before the exceptionally strong flax fibers can be spun into linen, they first have to be separated from the rest of the stalk in a process known as retting. The highest-quality linen is retted in slow-moving, natural water sources. European linens are among the finest in the world, with the French producing some of the whitest and most delicate of textiles.

Pat Camp scored this exceptional red-and-white tablecloth along with a dozen matching napkins at a New York flea market. White embroidery stitched inside the red outline of the many intricate details such as butterflies, flowers, and thistles adds important depth to the design.

Collecting European linens is an adored pastime and one that shop owner Pat Camp has enjoyed for 25 years. Her stunning collections lie heaped, layer upon layer, on the deep, wide shelves of the large walk-in closet she has dedicated to these treasures.

"Antique linens are so endearing and so enduring," says Pat, who searches for unique finds to add to her collection wherever she goes, whether it is to an antiques shop in America or a Monday flea market in Nice, France. One amazing day she even found herself in Geneva, Switzerland, when a French Countess was selling the exquisite linens from her household.

Bringing European linens across miles and time to our American homes adds elegance in a unique and lovely way.

Blue and white embroideries are very collectible. Blue embroidery threads were very difficult to acquire centuries ago. When a young lady had blue embroidery thread, she was fortunate. Today, blue threads come in a variety of shades. As shown above, displaying blue and white embroidered items in varying shades is stunning.

THE ALLURE
of *Silver*

Lovingly polished to a lustrous shine, this precious metal earns our enduring affection. Darkening crevices only enhance the appeal of antique silver, reminding collectors that the patina of age adds beauty to life's most cherished treasures.

Antique silver napkin rings do their duty as functional elements of a refined dinner setting by corralling cloth napkins, but these ornately engraved jewels of the tabletop stand alone as works of art in their own right. Fashioned circa 1865 to 1900, the napkin rings are from the collection of antiques dealer Carol O'Steen and include examples of English, American, Russian, German, and French craftsmanship.

Elegant ENGRAVING

Sterling silver imbues a home with the rich ambience of timeless grace. In the dining room, etched insignias on gleaming antique tea sets and polished serving trays lend a sense of tradition to modern interiors.

Opposite: This masterful hand-engraved and monogrammed American tea set dates back to 1900. Trailing vines and flowers bloom on the intricately etched surfaces—a testament to the precision skill of the gifted silversmith who created them. Above: A heavily embellished English tea service was crafted in 1870. Note the figural spouts on the teapot and the water pot, as well as the dainty flower knobs. The set is engraved with a triple monogram.

Personal
EFFECTS

An ornate hollowware mirror and vanity set from the Victorian era reflect an opulent time when a lady's dressing table showcased a perfumed oasis of cosmetics, jewelry, and pampering products.

"The dressing room of every well-bred woman should be both elegant and comfortable in proportion to her fortune and position," counsels Baroness Blanche Staffe in her 1893 etiquette manual, *The Lady's Dressing Room* (Dodo Press). "It may be simply comfortable if its owner cannot make it luxurious, but must be provided everything necessary for a careful toilette."

In Victorian times, the central element of a woman's personal space was her dressing table, appointed with a glittering assortment of tools and products she used for beautification. An intimate retreat reserved exclusively for the lady of the house, it bore the marks of her personality. The baroness encourages, "Everything placed upon it—brushes, combs, boxes, scent-bottles, etc.—should be chosen with artistic taste."

The vanity set, pictured left and opposite, presents a splendid example of the careful attention to detail applied to dressing-table accoutrements in this era. Boasting the world's largest inventory of new and old china, silver, and crystal, Replacements, Ltd., a Greensboro, North Carolina-based retailer, obtained this hollowware vanity set from a silver dealer in Massachusetts.

These pieces are from the pattern Lily, produced by the Whiting Manufacturing Company in New York City from 1902 to 1920. Wreaths of flowers frame hand-engraved monograms in this striking tableau.

The twelve-piece collection has been preserved in its entirety—a valuable acquisition, according to Jason Price, vice president of operations for Replacements: "Over time, the individual pieces in these estate silver vanity sets are often damaged or separated as a collection. In many cases, only the larger items, such as mirrors or brushes, survive wear and time. To come across a set with this many pieces that is in excellent condition is a rare find."

Opposite: A Victorian-era treasure, these stunning silver hollowware vanity accessories have been maintained in pristine condition. The twelve-piece set includes a hand mirror, shoehorn, nail file, cuticle knife, buttonhook, nail buffer, hair receiver jar, dresser jar, hairbrush, clothes brush, and two cosmetic jars.

Engraved with the letters JES in a feathered script, this silver coffee and tea service displays the expert craftsmanship of colonial silversmiths. Opposite: An elegant set of monogrammed silver salvers dating from 1765 to 1772 lay hidden for nearly two hundred years.

The Fanciful Monograms of
COLONIAL WILLIAMSBURG

Carefully curated relics displayed in this preserved Virginia settlement reveal perceptions of the colonial lifestyle, with personal emblems on many discoveries enabling historians to trace the lineage of some of the earliest American pioneers.

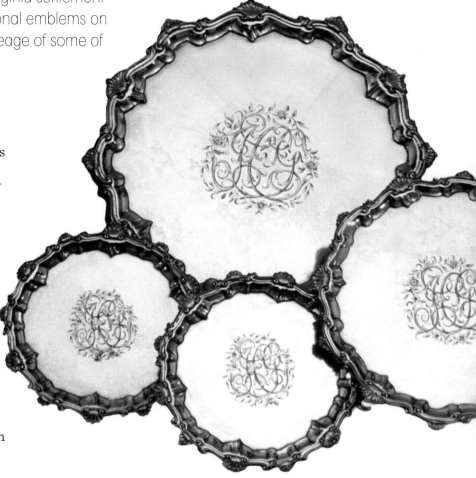

The DeWitt Wallace Decorative Arts Museum in Colonial Williamsburg offers glimpses of Virginia's earliest settlers through acquisitions such as a set of antique English silver salvers, right, and a silver coffee and tea set, opposite.

The salvers were part of a silver cache belonging to North Carolina merchant Josiah Granberry and his wife, Christian. London silversmith Ebenezer Coker crafted the two smallest salvers circa 1766 and the largest salver in approximately 1769. John Carter, also a London silversmith, made the largest salver circa 1769. Remarkably similar despite their different makers, all four ornately rimmed plates bear the engraved cipher JCG.

Viewing the salvers, one can almost feel the heightened sense of apprehension that pervaded this settlement on April 18, 1775. News of an impending British invasion spread quickly through the colonies, prompting many to hide their valuables in preparation for the battles to come. The Granberrys buried their silver more than two centuries ago in Nansemond County, Virginia, on the eve of the Revolutionary War, and the cache was unearthed in 1961.

Connecting tourists to happier occasions, the silver coffee and tea service reveals the artfulness of colonial silversmiths. With their curving forms, fine engraving, and handsome finials, the items represent the highest achievement in size and complexity for silversmiths of the day. Captain John Stone and Elizabeth Keeling, of Norfolk, Virginia, commissioned the set in 1799, in celebration of their nuptials. John A. Schanck, of New York City, fashioned the coffeepot, and Jeremiah Andrews of Norfolk, Virginia, retailed the piece. Andrews designed the teapot, creamer, sugar dish, and waste bowl to coordinate with the coffeepot. Although the coffeepot's form and finial vary from the other pieces, the feathered-script monogram unifies the set.

Purchased by The Colonial Williamsburg Foundation, these silver artifacts offer a gleaming connection to early American history.

Carol O'Steen: STERLING IMPRESSIONS

More than four decades after she established a thriving antiques business in Florida, this dealer of distinctive and discontinued silver still enjoys the exhilaration of discovering extraordinary vintage pieces.

For Carol O'Steen, the joy of the hunt for unusual silver pieces has never lost its luster. Carol opened Unique Silver in the 1970s, when her family bought a 5,400-square-foot house in Marianna, Florida. Built in 1904, the Italianate home with a charming widow's walk was zoned for commercial use, so she allocated extra space for an antiques shop.

In spotting vintage wares she could not identify, Carol and her husband, Rip, also found a passion for exploring their past. "In the process, we became intrigued with silver," she explains. "We learned about hallmarks, silversmiths, and the many countries that have produced sterling and coin silver. A single piece of silver may have a delightful history; you just have to take the time to investigate." She narrowed the shop's focus to distinctive and discontinued silver flatware and hollowware.

Carol remembers the thrill of a North Carolina attic find: "We acquired a cloth bundle of feathered clipper-script-style monogrammed teaspoons with an ink-written note stating that the teaspoons were used in the governor's mansion and came from Governor Stokes's wife's family." Research confirmed that Montfort Stokes was elected governor of North Carolina in 1830 and that silversmith W. Pearce worked in Virginia during this time.

The entrepreneur holds an affinity for Early American coin silver, which was created before 1865. "When settlers first came to America," she explains, "silversmiths brought tools and knowledge but no silver. All we had were coins for trade, as there were no silver mines east of the Mississippi River." Silversmithing provided itinerant work during those days. Most families acquired silver a little at a time, and pieces varied by weight, depending upon the coins that could be spared. Customers had the freedom to conceive their own patterns, incorporating their choice of motifs and engravings into the design.

Since the O'Steens relocated to Tallahassee in 1991, Carol has continued to operate Unique Silver locally by appointment, and she interacts with a wide base of customers nationwide through e-mail and telephone exchanges. She maintains a "want list" and corresponds with collectors when she comes across desirable pieces. Carol and Rip operate a booth at the monthly Scott Antique Markets in Atlanta, Georgia, and they are vendors at the semiannual Marburger Farm Antique Show in Round Top, Texas.

Opposite and above: This 1913 silver baby cup features stunning hand-engraved details. The feathered clipper-script monogram, draped floral garland, and lacy etchings demonstrate the silversmith's expertise. The front of the cup bears the child's monogram, while the bottom of the mug notes the cipher of the godfather who commissioned the gift. Right: English and American napkin rings created circa 1880 to 1950 range in value from approximately $200 to $350. Vintage silver dealer Carol O'Steen offers more than six hundred of these collectibles and searches continually for new monograms to add to her inventory. Clients report using monogrammed napkin rings during dinner parties to spark conversation, asking guests to create personas inspired by the initials engraved on theirs.

The Treasured Patina of
THE SILVER MARKET

With an eye toward strengthening the bonds of family while preserving precious remembrances from the past, the owner of this quaint Fairhope, Alabama, shop celebrates the art of the table and the joy of treasured times shared around it.

Growing up in a military family that moved frequently, the constant for P.J. Bass McAleer was gathering around the dinner table together. "It felt like we were home when the barrels of china, crystal, and silver arrived at the new base," she remembers. "One of my favorite childhood memories is of standing at the kitchen sink, slowly hand washing and rinsing silver, crystal, and china and admiring the beauty of each piece."

In 1981, the escalating price of silver bullion inspired P.J. to open The Silver Market in Fairhope, Alabama, in an effort to protect precious heirlooms from being sold and melted down. She relocated the store to its current setting in 1995, a charming 1,800-square-foot cottage surrounded by lush palmettos, a Chinese fan palm, native plants, and a garden of herbs and lettuces.

Offering a treasury of antiques dating primarily from the early nineteenth century to the World War I era, the proprietress describes the shop as "a lifestyle store." Along with other vintage finds such as collectibles, china, lace, and linen, P.J.'s inventory includes a vast array of silver flatware and hollowware. She is quick to point out that the heirloom items she sells are not

museum quality. Their intended use is to enhance the beauty of life's most meaningful occasions. "Our mission is not just to reclaim artifacts," she notes. "The tradition of bonding with family and friends is at the heart of what we do."

In today's hectic, fast-paced world, P.J. fears that our society is becoming increasingly fragmented when it comes to spending quality time with loved ones, which is why she delights in the conviviality The Silver Market's collectibles inspire. "It's important to slow down, to share, and to enjoy conversations at the table," she maintains. "Sitting down together and sharing what you have is the greatest expression of love."

The beach-resort town of Fairhope draws visitors from around the world, and through the years, many returning shop patrons have forged close friendships with P.J. and her staff. "It is a very personal process helping people choose a gift for someone they love. They want to find something that really expresses their relationship with the recipient," P.J. says. "Our clients have an eye for beauty and a deep understanding of history. They are preservationists of both material culture and the culture of family."

A fresh-cut bouquet spills from this lovely hand-pierced, sterling-silver flower basket created circa 1910 by Reed & Barton. Opposite, top left: A petite velvet-lined antique English spectacles case invites a closer look. Opposite, top right: This exquisite sterling-silver ladies purse from the end of the nineteenth century is ornamented front and back with acid-etched motifs. A hand-engraved monogram provides the culminating detail.

Rendered in whispers of white-on-white, these embroidered linens speak to the preferences of their owners. A classic block-letter monogram stitched in a frame conveys an appreciation for timeless tradition, while a gently curving script reveals a love of feminine details. A simple piece of linen becomes a canvas for personal expression when embroidered with letters thoughtfully combined to form a unique symbol of self.

Personally YOURS

Monograms mark many cherished treasures, whether sentimental household items bearing our own initials or objects commemorating milestone moments, imprinted with the ciphers of people we love. Custom emblems proclaim the dignity of me, the commitment of us, and the celebration of you.

PERSONALLY SPEAKING

Tracing initials that have left indelible impressions in her life, *Victoria* Editor-in-Chief Phyllis DePiano reflects on her abiding love for monograms.

TEXT BY PHYLLIS DEPIANO

My affinity for personalization began in my early teen years, when the most sought-after accessory among my girlfriends was a certain brand of leather purse. Although I longed to own the status item, it was not possible on the spending money I earned babysitting and playing piano at church. I received the coveted bag, complete with my initials, as a Christmas gift from my parents that year, and my enchantment with monograms ensued.

As a young woman refining my personal tastes, I took note of renowned insignias of the fashion industry: the entwining Cs of the House of Chanel, the interlocking LV made famous by Louis Vuitton, and the legendary Gs of Gucci. Customers and collectors alike prize these iconic symbols highly. Entire businesses have been built around the monograms of their founders. These celebrated tastemakers show us that a well-thought-out cipher encapsulates an individual's unique essence.

My husband, Neal, and I began a quest to create a custom insignia when we married seven years ago. Calligrapher Allison Banks designed our hand-drawn monogram as a wedding gift. We loved the symbolism of layering our initials to create a formal emblem. Allison rendered sketches, tweaking details with each version until the design perfectly expressed our vision. Because my husband's first name and my maiden name both begin with an N, I can use our monogram for us or for me.

Frequent visits to the Biltmore estate in Asheville, North Carolina, inspired us to adopt acorns and oak leaves as our family symbol. We incorporated this biblical motif into a second casual monogram designed by Angela Atherton. Branches representing strength and growth wrap our two initials in a pledge for an enduring marriage.

The highly detailed combination of letters comprising our formal monogram is centered, white-on-white, on hemstitched place mats. Opposite: The same symbol was worked on russet napkins chosen to accent our monogrammed china by Bernardaud (pictured right.) Opposite top: A rubber stamp etched with our symbol is useful for embellishing note cards and paper goods, including gift wrap. Opposite bottom: My formal monogram is hand-engraved on a gold rope-edged disk, shown with a custom cigar-band ring etched with my casual monogram and a gold-ribbon script ring. (Douglas R. Harris Jewelers in North Carolina created the pieces.)

In recent years, I have had the pleasure of viewing some of the most exquisite ciphers embroidered on linen, engraved on silver, and painted on china. I have studied the tentative stitching of antique schoolgirl samplers and marveled at the intricacy of vintage letterforms. And just as that young girl of long ago was awestruck to discover her initials imprinted on a leather purse, a beautiful monogram still stops me in my tracks and makes me pause to study the details.

Why not establish your own monogram style? Personalization was a labor of love or a gift of great expense in times past. Today, we are fortunate that we can obtain these items with ease. Neal and I have made our home a personal haven by incorporating our cipher into the décor, and my heart still skips a beat to see our initials entwined. Like us, you might want to have more than one monogram, depending upon the occasion or application. Whether your tastes lean toward elegant and traditional, sleek and modern, or somewhere in between, I encourage you to develop a monogram that expresses your style in a manner that is uniquely you.

Innovative
INSIGNIA TRADITIONS

Rendered in shades of blue, this cipher embodies a masculine approach to monogramming. The classic emblem, designed by Jessica Stalnaker of Empress Stationery, offers inventive possibilities for presentation.

Timeless letterforms combine to fashion a distinguished monogram for a man. Depending upon the application, the design can be large or small, with one color or two, and with wreath and cipher used together or separately. Opposite: Complementary embroidery enhances this linen place mat. Computer programs allow personalization of paper goods, such as wrapping paper and envelope seals. Left: For a sweet finish to a celebratory meal, serve individual cakes with the guest of honor's monogram piped in swirls of buttercream icing.

MRS. WILLIAM
T THE HONOUR OF
MARRIAGE OF T

manda R
to

with Seare

tails, Dinner an
AFTER FIVE O'C
COTTISH
NOR

Allison Banks:
INITIAL SUCCESS

Combining innate creative ability, an artistic heritage, and the desire to leave a lasting impression, this talented calligrapher makes her mark fashioning bespoke monograms and custom stationery.

Born into a family of artists and craftsmen, Birmingham, Alabama, native Allison R. Banks felt the pull toward creative pursuits early on. At 15, she took a part-time job with Bob Rosser, a well-known engraver and friend of the family. The teenager answered phones during the Christmas rush but sketched during her downtime. Rosser took note of Allison's talent and became her mentor.

Although her parents and Rosser saw a potential career in calligraphy for her, Allison initially resisted:

"I will never do this full time." She embarked on a decadelong career in publishing but could not quell a lingering desire to create objects of permanence. She remembers, "I didn't always feel like what I was doing would stick around for fifty years. There was something in me that wanted to create a legacy."

Through freelance calligraphy work, a constant since college, Allison discovered that her greatest sense of fulfillment comes from designing details that leave indelible memories. "Think back to a big event," she

points out, "and you'll probably find a note, an invitation, or a symbol that helps mark that moment. It's amazing how the little things stay with us.

"Creating something beautiful with my hands was appealing," the calligrapher continues. "And like other craftsmen who work in wood, metal, or clay, I learned that my designs could last generations if given the right attention and care."

Allison began to realize that few people design one-of-a-kind monograms. The stationery industry was changing, she observed, and there was a need for hand-drawn work. She started developing her own way of doing things that blended old and new.

Despite steady growth in commissioned projects and an ever-widening circle of clients, the entrepreneur says it took a leap of faith to pursue her passion for calligraphy full time. As she reflects on her business, Allison R. Banks Designs, launched five years ago, Allison credits experience in other artistic fields with leading her to this point. "If I had tried this six or seven years ago, it wouldn't have worked because the time wasn't right," she admits. "I can look back and see how my style, eye, and craftsmanship are better now. My career path helped prepare me for this work."

To create a custom monogram, the artist begins with a consultation. Just as handwriting says a lot about a person, she explains, a monogram says so much—clients need to look inside themselves to discover their personalities.

Pencil sketches refine the design, and upon approval, Allison renders the final version in ink. Each hand-drawn insignia is distinct. Even when people find in her gallery styles they favor, she never duplicates a design. "It's just like commissioning a painting," she says. "All the monograms are original."

Customers receive a scan of the initial ink sketch, along with high-resolution computer files. Many engaged couples debut their new insignia at their wedding, incorporating the symbol into stationery, giftware, and more. One couple had their monogram re-created in an ice bar for the reception, while another had theirs stenciled onto chocolate-truffle favors. One clever bride had hers embroidered on one hundred linen cocktail napkins to use for the festivities and to keep for the rest of her life.

In addition to monograms, Allison's calligraphy work graces invitations, menus, envelopes, escort cards, and place cards. An in-house wedding line is in the works, with other projects to follow.

The calligrapher says her biggest reward comes in knowing she is creating a family heritage. Many wedding clients have returned to request ciphers for their offspring, and Allison says she anticipates bringing the process full circle. "I look forward to the day when children of clients start coming back to have me design a wedding monogram."

Opposite: Allison's hand-drawn insignia is the core symbol of her business, but designing it was an arduous task. "It took a year to really settle on one that represents me," she says. This page: A couple's monogram marks napkins and envelope labels for their nuptials.

Sarah and Francis
11·17·12

Before & AFTER

Vintage linens become uniquely yours when stitched with your initials. Thoughtful selections blend beautiful, old textiles with new machine embroidery to create personal treasures enriched with a sense of history.

Fragile linens cannot withstand machine stitching, but sturdier textiles can be embroidered with stabilizers to protect the fibers of the cloth. Opposite bottom, left and right: An existing emblem on this hemstitched towel encircles a monogram sized to fit the frame. Opposite, top left and center left: Exquisite pale peach linen place mats are enhanced with the addition of a large initial. The cream-colored thread and ornate letter style complement the lace border perfectly, seamlessly blending old and new. This page: A lavish C takes center stage on a damask napkin.

Signature Dishes:
HAND-PAINTED CHINA

Cultivate an elegant table with antique plates featuring stunning monograms.
Searching for particular letters provides a rewarding treasure hunt, but personalized
china can be appreciated merely for the artistic rendering of the emblems.

Above left: Painted ciphers on the lids coordinate
with the slim gold handles and rims that accent the
understated design of these covered casserole dishes.
Above right: A bulbous teapot, creamer, and covered
sugar bowl rest on slender pedestals banded in gold.
The formal monogram is duplicated on other pieces in
the set. Left and opposite: Embellished with an elaborate
rendering of the original owner's initials, these scalloped-
edged vintage plates create a lovely, sophisticated
tablescape. Discovering a complete service of
monogrammed china at an antiques store is a find
worth savoring, even if the initials are not your own.

PASSIONATE
LINEN PURSUITS

Esteemed for both their beauty and function, embroidered textiles impart a gracious sense of welcome to interiors. The joy of collecting springs from acquiring magnificent but discarded linens and restoring their purpose as beloved home elements for use and display.

138 Monograms & Antique Linens

Fresh linens are kept ready for service within this treasury of well-organized textiles.

United by a common letter and color palette, this tableau of monogrammed tea towels comprises textiles of different styles and eras. From the casual simplicity of an eyelet-trimmed towel draped in a basket to the more formal lace-edged linens on the shelf, the white-on-white ensemble presents a cohesive display. The interpretation of the initial H varies from classic to ornate in this sampling of embroidery techniques, but the expertise of the handwork unifies the collection.

This page: Embroidered towels drape a vintage cupboard in supple elegance, offering a soft counterpoint to the rustic painted wood of the cabinet. The snowy-white linen highlights the owner's charming cache of bucolic figurines, which contribute a gentle nod to the pleasures of country life. Opposite: Too beautiful to be tucked into a drawer and forgotten, this array of tea towels brings beauty to daily life. Contrasting fabrics and variations in embroidery and trim add interest to the assortment.

This page: An immaculate collection of white-on-white linens emphasizes variations in artistic letterform styles and exquisite embroidery techniques. The needleworker's meticulous attention to the stitchery is spotlighted amidst alabaster fields of fabric. The ease of machine embroidery allowed elegant personalization of these new linens, from tea towels to pillowcases, with letters chosen for their beauty. Opposite: Scripted initials rendered in cheerful red and French blue embroidery threads enhance tea towels in a cozy kitchen.

Love Letters

It is the ultimate romantic gesture and a sense of great pride for a beautiful bride to show her new initials after she has married. Symbolic of the intertwining of two lives, monogramming provides the perfect opportunity to debut the new insignia.

TEXT BY PHYLLIS DEPIANO

Every bride wants her day to be uniquely hers and to show her style. "My dress was my 'something old' and my 'something new,'" says Katie Hoffman of her wedding gown. Katie loves classic fashion, and when she discovered this vintage wedding gown from the 1970s, she was thrilled to think that it could be remade into a more current style with the vintage lace and fabrics preserved.

The original gown was disassembled, and a new bodice was created with the original lace and fabrics. The skirt was the original skirt with every piece of lace still intact. The newly created train was inserted into the back of the skirt, carefully overlapping the old laces with the new. Central to the train was Katie's new initials embroidered in tone-on-tone antique white. "My sisters loved the dress, and the monogram was placed at the base of the train so that their monograms could be added to the dress if they choose to wear the dress for their weddings," Katie says with delight. The monogram was stitched to the top layer of organza fabric so that others could be added easily.

Katie's sister Margaret presented her with a vintage hankie bearing a beautifully embroidered K for the wedding day. The delicate stitches are so feminine, making it a perfect gift for Katie.

Kelly Harrington purchased her dress and veil and wanted her new initials on her veil for her special day. Her veil was very long and had a beautiful shape at the base for initials. Since the veil was wedding-day-ready, her initials were stitched on a separate piece of tulle, edged with matching lace, and then sewn to the veil.

The lace medallion is a very simple way to apply a monogram to a veil. Working with tulle can be very challenging unless the proper stabilizer is used for embroidery. By working on a separate medallion, several different types of lettering styles can be stitched and the perfect one selected. All three of her letters are very flowing and curvy, making a beautiful monogram. As is the custom, her new last name initial was in the center, larger than the flanking first name initial on the left and the maiden name initial on the right.

Cynthia Nouri founded her company, Sasha Nicholas, out of her love of dinnerware and beautiful china. New brides cherish the custom pieces she designs, which mark the start of a new life together as husband and wife. Couples can create their own tableware and choose the perfect color for their own cipher.

One of the most endearing pieces is the personalized plate with a handwritten message on the back. A mother's hand-written note was made into the china plate, shown above, by Cynthia and her team. What bride wouldn't love a personal note from a mother or grandmother on her special day?

Sasha Nicholas china is carried by specialty retailers, and couples can register for this as their main china pattern. The monogrammed salad plates can be paired with other china patterns, shown left. Brides that inherit family dinnerware often will have salad plates made with their new monogram to update their collection for their new family. Whether you are looking for a gift of one unique piece or a full set of china, Sasha Nicholas's variety of china patterns and monogram styles is the perfect source.

The beautiful bride shows off her new china with a chic cobalt blue monogram.

Sasha Nicholas napkin rings are prized by anyone who loves a beautiful table setting. The unique lettering styles and color choices allow you to mix-and-match for your individual look.

For Meaghan Davis Kinkade's wedding day, her new initials were beautifully stitched onto the wide silk ribbon of her bouquet. Her dress was classic and sleek, and the ornate monogram was the perfect touch.

Christened INSIGNIAS

An heirloom-style christening gown befittingly honors a celebrated new addition. Delicate details seem to whisper in sweet serenade, "You are cherished, beloved baby of mine. Welcome to our family."

Opposite: Ruffles of vintage French lace lend provenance to a newly constructed baby gown of off-white Swiss batiste. Machine embroidery stitched in thread to match the lace adorns the skirt with an elegant monogram and graceful flourishes. Above right: Bullion roses and narrow lace trim the bodice. Below left: A length of leftover lace provides the perfect width to make a matching bonnet, softly gathered with a generous length of ivory silk-satin ribbon.

The fit of a christening gown is judged by the bodice and not the skirt. The highly dramatic drapes of fabric in this long skirt hang perfectly from the detailed bodice. With its portrait neckline, the lacework is showcased on the bodice. The little sleeves receive gathered rows of lace aligned with the shoulder seams.

Each skirt panel flares into godets and is bordered by lace connecting each panel. On the back of the skirt, the birthdate is embroidered in the center motif. Each panel terminates into a scalloped hem finished with entredeux and gathered lace.

When Connie Palmer designed this christening gown, the center of this creation was a monogrammed oval comprised of carefully placed motifs surrounding the letter trio. On either side of the oval are rows of scalloped lace drawing attention to the magnificence of the center panel.

Enchantment can begin with a glance. One
arresting example of stitchery can spark a
fascination with needlework, while a single
piece of extravagantly edged cloth can
inspire an infatuation with linens. This beguiling
trio of vintage handkerchiefs ornamented with
padded satin stitching might kindle a lifetime
passion for collecting.

Preserving
A HERITAGE

Artfully embroidered linens wrap a home in the gentility of timeless grace. Employed daily and consistently well maintained, today's thoughtfully curated textiles will appreciate in value, becoming tomorrow's treasured heirlooms.

A MODERN LINEN
Trousseau

Today's bride generally amasses a collection of household linens quickly during her engagement. But applying the forethought of the conventional trousseau ensures a well-appointed treasury of textiles that will serve the long-term needs of a growing family.

For centuries, tradition decreed that daughters accumulate a trousseau—the word derived from a French term meaning "to bundle." Early in her life, a girl was gifted a linen press for storing household textiles she made or collected during her youth. Set aside for her future marriage, a classic trousseau contained all the soft necessities a proper lady needed to set up housekeeping.

In the fourteenth century, the utilitarian trousseau included a modest collection of household linens and clothing. But by the nineteenth century, the concept had grown to encompass an impressive abundance of linens, their fine quality and intricate adornments a mark of social standing for the wealthiest Victorian families. The rise of popular fashion during this era tempted women to update their wardrobes frequently, so by the twentieth century, the bridal trousseau had narrowed to comprise only household items and underclothes.

In the modern age, instead of compiling a linen trousseau during adolescence, a bride generally gathers household articles in the months leading up to her wedding. A thoughtfully selected registry can help loved ones shower a bride and groom with textiles that will not only endure throughout their marriage but bless future generations as well.

Couples are wise to buy the best linens they can afford, bearing in mind that an initial investment in first-rate quality will pay off in years of durability. White and off-white are classically elegant color choices, and pairing neutral fabrics with subtle details such as hemstitching and tone-on-tone embroidery ensures that basic linens will complement a home's décor throughout the years as tastes and trends evolve.

A well-stocked linen closet helps a household run smoothly and encourages hospitality, but care should be taken to avoid accumulating so many varieties that linens suffer from disuse. For everyday items such as sheets and towels, collecting three sets for each member of the household allows uninterrupted flow, with one set in use, one in the laundry, and one in the cupboard. A few aprons, ten to fifteen dish towels, and a dozen or so dishcloths should suffice for the kitchen.

In the dining room, a simple white linen or brocade tablecloth with an 8-inch drop and a dozen matching napkins will suit a range of occasions, from formal to casual. A single tablecloth provides a good starting point for a new hostess. Additional table linens—and the decision to collect more—should reflect the couple's aesthetic and entertaining style. Some contemporary couples shun table linens because of their upkeep, but many easy-care fabrics do not require ironing and

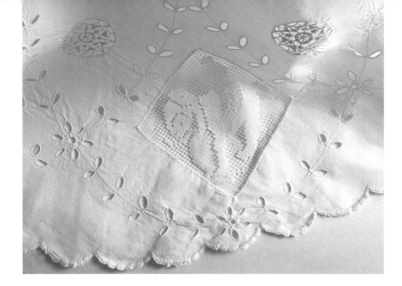

prove to be economical, environmentally responsible solutions for daily use. And the superior charms of fine linens to disposable tableware simply cannot be denied. A tasteful collection of cloth table runners, place mats, tablecloths, and napkins imparts a bounty of inspiration for tablescapes that reflect the seasons, boost conviviality at holiday gatherings, and bring a sense of celebration to everyday meals.

With a third of our lives spent in dreamy slumber, bed linens merit the greatest allocation of a household-linen budget. Finely spun combed cotton with a thread count between 200 and 400 creates an inviting cocoon of comfort. Well-worn linen sheets offer a refreshing oasis from summer heat, while luxurious fabrics such as silk and satin beckon with a sumptuous escape from the cares of the day. It is wise to keep an extra set of favorite sheets in reserve to avoid losing sleep over the frayed hem of a top sheet or a tear in the fitted sheet. In warm climates, a richly patterned matelassé coverlet blankets a bed in traditional elegance, and a quilt folded across the foot guards against an unexpected chill. For cooler regions, a classic duvet embellished with embroidery and fluffed with a comforter coaxes a peaceful night's rest.

Other household linens such as throw pillows, decorative comforters and pillow shams, blankets, slipcovers, draperies, tea towels, and doilies adorn a house with soft whispers of welcome. These supple accents cost little to make or purchase, so they can be replaced seasonally or as styles change.

Today's bride may find that obtaining a linen trousseau kindles a lifelong passion for collecting and using exquisite textiles to enrich the beauty of her home and enhance the experience of daily life.

Monogram
EXPRESSION

Let your imagination be your guide when selecting letter styles that express personality and preference. Consider how the textile will be used when choosing placement. Traditionally folded napkins bear vertical letters, while those used in napkin rings are embellished diagonally.

Delicate stitchery in pink thread marks the bedding in a little girl's room. Monograms were stitched high on Euro shams so they are visible above decorative toile pillows.

This page: Rich embroidery coordinates with cranberry dining-room walls. Opposite: An initial provides the finishing detail on purchased napkins with a fleur-de-lis motif.

Bold colors and clever placement update traditional linens. From left to right: Blue-striped French kitchen linens get a boost from playful red letters. Centered for display within the folded square, an inventive cipher offers a modern alternative to a conventional three-letter monogram. Opposite page: The large scale of a vivid monogram creates a striking look.

A collection of old linens with delicate hand-sewn lettering serves as inspiration for new monograms. The traditional colors have given way to new, vibrant motifs and lettering. Amy Gray of Bobbins Design creates new, fresh monograms for young couples wishing to embrace tradition yet make their own style statements.

Classic
WHITE-ON-WHITE

Amy Gray of Bobbins Design was challenged with a lovely project for a Mother-of-the-Bride. While searching for a lovely tablecloth to use at her daughter's wedding, she purchased a vintage cloth with initials in two of the corners. She brought the cloth to Amy who selected a beautiful, larger embroidery lettering style and stitched the daughter's new monogram on a corner. When the second daughter marries, her initials will take their place in the remaining corner. An exquisite vintage heirloom became part of another family's heirloom collection, marking the weddings of two daughters. The cloth was used at the bride's cake table.

"White-on-white is timeless. With every monogram I stitch, I am creating heirlooms that will be passed to future generations."

—AMY GRAY

A classic white-on-white monogram newly created is the perfect gift for a new bride. This page, the new monogram was stitched on vintage damask napkins. There are numerous design styles with classic shapes and embellishments that are perfectly suited for vintage linens. Shown on opposite page, the monograms are new styles stitched on new linens. A linen wardrobe is always a welcomed gift in any household.

Treasured reminders of long-ago days, when every lady carried a handkerchief, these pristine linen squares were personalized for the original owner. Delicately stitched monograms are surrounded by an array of motifs created by hand using only a needle and thread. A charming gift for any bride is a vintage handkerchief with her new initial.

Of REST *and*
RESTORATION

In a journey that reads more like a novel than a business plan, Pandora de Balthazár has followed her heart from a bucolic childhood in the Deep South, across oceans to distant palaces, and back home to discover her true purpose.

TEXT BY MELISSA LESTER
PHOTOGRAPHY STEPHANIE WELBOURNE
STYLING KATHLEEN COOK AND MISSIE NEVILLE CRAWFORD

This page: When Pandora de Balthazár debuted her European Sleep System, the bed pillows did not fit standard American shams. An avid linen collector, she began selling antique pillow slips, thus introducing consumers to the quality and exquisite loveliness of textiles previously unavailable in this country. "Some people find us, attracted by the beauty," the entrepreneur says. "Others understand our message of nurturing and seek us out."

Pandora de Balthazár, founder of the luxury-bedding company that bears her name, has been known to linger for hours with guests who visit her retail space in Pensacola, Florida. In a role she describes as equal parts therapist and interior designer, the former financial planner says she now helps clients invest in their own well-being.

With roots in Dalton, Georgia, which she calls the "textile capital of the new world," Pandora grew up with an appreciation of handmade goods. She compares her rural upbringing, where from a tender age she was trained to sew and embroider, with the traditional education common to generations of young women raised abroad.

During her international travels, Pandora amassed an impressive collection of linens, prized as much for their practicality as for their artistry. She learned to distinguish antique from vintage textiles—whether primitive or refined, finely wrought pieces boast a heavier weight and superior craftsmanship, she notes. Realistic motifs rendered in meticulous stitches typify these finds, which often tell a story.

Opposite: A circa-1840 handmade Swiss tablecloth enhances this elegant setting. Fine stitching, perfectly designed portraiture and cutwork, and filet-lace edging make a gracious statement for entertaining. Right: These alabaster napkins feature Appenzell embroidery—a style of whitework that originated in Northeast Switzerland and includes openwork backgrounds, floral motifs, and occasionally figures.

In the midst of a successful career working with closely held corporations, a serious automobile accident taught the jet-setting adviser the importance of creating a personal sanctuary. Following medical treatment in Hungary, Pandora convalesced for six months within a lavish nineteenth-century castle, where she realized the restorative power of sleep. Much of the healing she credits to cushions arranged to cradle her frame—a precursor to the popular European Sleep System she later developed.

In 1995, Pandora had just returned to the United States when, again, her life shifted dramatically. Her family's beachfront house and almost all their possessions were lost when Hurricane Opal struck Pensacola. With no idea where the path would lead, Pandora took a leap of faith when a woman who had heard about her Hungarian pillows invited her to become a vendor at High Point Market—the largest trade show in the furnishings industry.

This page: A custom headboard provides a serene backdrop for a mix of delicate bed covers. Opposite, Left to Right: Scarlet threads in this striking ensemble capture attention. Giving the boudoir accents of seasonal color is as easy as exchanging lengths of ribbon.

Opposite: The company's in-house seamstresses combine favorite images and seventeenth- and eighteenth-century letterforms to create bespoke monograms, executed with multicolored, padded, or even metallic stitchery. This page: An array of decorative cushions from around the world feature a range of distinctive patterns.

Nearly twenty years later, the Pandora de Balthazár company offers an ethereal selection of antique and custom-made sheets, shams, coverlets, and tablecloths, as well as foundational elements for the boudoir. Merchandise can be perused at prominent antiques shows around the country, as well as at the business's Florida location.

The purveyor of European linens encourages customers to embrace a more graceful way of living. "So many women need to be nurtured, and they don't even know it," she says—a lesson Pandora learned years ago   and a gift she shares with all who seek repose amidst her exquisite wares.

Delicate antique linen hand towels display tone-on-tone pink in feminine script styles. The owner of this pale pink collection collects linens without regard to the initials they bear.

CHANGING
COLORS

Although white embroidery on white linen is a historically favored
selection, color updates traditional textiles with a rainbow of potential
combinations in hues that are certain to please today's collectors.

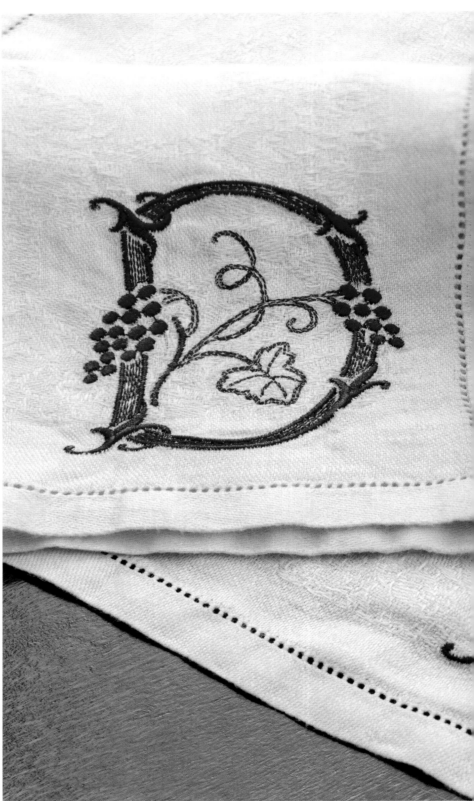

Opposite, far left: PDN looks updated yet classic when embroidered in French blue. Center: Color lends a casual interpretation to classic insignias with thread chosen to suit the table setting, dining room, or specific occasion. Stitched in burgundy for a holiday affair, this fanciful D adds vibrant contrast to hemstitched napkins. Rendered in peach for a ladies' luncheon, as displayed above, the same design appears more demure. Below: These napkins demonstrate the transformative effects of color. Fashionable robin's-egg blue modernizes a classic rendering of KHE.

CREATING YOUR OWN STYLE

With the advent of modern day home sewing and embroidery machines, you can create your own linen collection by purchasing monogram designs and embroidering your own linens.

Sonia Showalter Designs is a company that designs monograms for machine embroidery for sewists who want to do their own monogramming. Many people are opting to monogram their own linens and select monograms from those commercially available. Sonia's monogram designs offer single initials surrounded by seasonal motifs or flourishes. For the sewist today, monogram designs can be downloaded to an embroidery sewing machine, and very quickly a set of beautiful linens can be created.

Just as the French introduced colored monograms and linens centuries ago, monograms using colored threads are very popular now, especially when surrounded by motifs that capture the spirit of the season. Just as formal china and informal everyday dishes have taken on bright colors and patterns, so have monogrammed linens and monograms.

Linens are very easy to care for today, and having many sets to use throughout the seasons is common. The traditional white-on-white will always be appropriate, but the festive initials on linens make wonderful gifts for a new bride.

Holiday linens are becoming fashionable when entertaining during the season. Incorporating holiday motifs with a monogram is not only beautiful but also gives your table settings a personal touch. Large families will sometimes use a single initial letter so that linens may be shared.

The monogram with a grapevine entwined is clever for wine and cheese parties. Why not have a set of napkins designated for wine tastings? Monogramming, which was once only reserved for professionals, is now available for home sewists as well. A wardrobe of monogrammed linens can be created using your own sewing machine and linens.

MONOGRAM PLACEMENT

Whether your choice of monograms is a single initial or multiple entwined initials, there are some basic placement guidelines worth considering.

Monograms are as personal as a signature. Whether the initials are wrapped in scrolls and flourishes or are plain in appearance, our monograms give a glimpse into our personalities.

The type of lettering you select is important as well. What is appropriate for a 25-year-old lady might be a little too much for a newborn. Oftentimes the size of the lettering will make the difference.

There is an abundance of embroidery styles and fonts created especially for our sewing machines. Equally important are beautifully hand embroidered monograms. These lovely examples from decades ago are highly collectible today. The hours spent embroidering can only be appreciated by one that has done embroidery. Our machines today can do the job in just minutes creating beautiful embellishments to linens and garments.

The proper placement of the letters is important, especially when you are presenting a gift.

There are traditional guidelines that you may want to consider when creating your personal monogram. These are guidelines only, as today creativity seems to trump tradition.

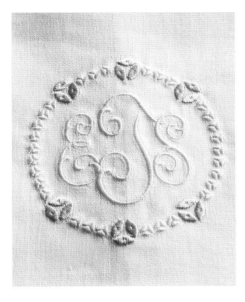

When initials appear the same size, then they are placed in order.

If you choose a monogram style with the larger letter in the center, the initial representing your last name appears in the middle flanked by your first name initial on the left and your middle (or maiden name) on the right.

If just one letter is being used then the initial representing the last name is selected.

A COUPLE'S MONOGRAM

When a monogram represents the man and wife then the initials are used together. The last name initial is larger and placed in the center. The wife's first name initial is on the left, and the husband's first name initial is on the right.

Typically a couple's monogram is used on linens, stationery, china, and anything that would be used representing both of them. This tradition began in the mid-nineteenth century and remains customary today.

An alternative to the three-letter monogram is the overlaid two-letter monogram. Symbolizing the union of two families, the last initials of the couple were interlaced or entwined to celebrate the marriage.

There are elaborate entwining monograms designed today using the first initials and the last initial of a couple. And with the hyphenating names and multiple names that are socially correct, monograms can be several letters entwined, creating a beautiful work of art that is personally yours.

Purveyors of
Fine Linens, Embroidery, and Monograms

Pat Kerr of Pat Kerr Designs is the known for her love of antique and vintage laces. Her one-of-a-kind wedding and christening gowns are sought after worldwide. *www.patkerr.com*

Robin Molbert is the proprietor of the online shop Fleur d'Andeol. Her bountiful collection of antique linens is always highly sought after by people who love exquisite linens. *www.fleurdandeol.com*

Beth Claybourn of Beth Claybourn Interiors uses antique linens in her beautiful interior design work. *www.bethclaybourninteriors.com*

Carolyn Gallier of CaroLinens is the online shopkeeper of vintage handkerchiefs and linens. *www.carolinens.com*

Sandy Patterson is the proprietor of High Cotton Ltd. the renowned shop in Williamsburg, VA, filled with antique and vintage linens, china, crystal, and silver. *www.highcottonwilliamsburg.com*

Pat Camp's love for beautiful linens is shared at Thompson House Antiques.

Carol O'Steen of Unique Silver offers an extensive selection of silver napkin rings as well as other beautiful silver pieces. *www.exceptionalsilver.com*

P.J. Bass McAleer of the Silver Market in Fairhope, AL features vintage linens, silver, laces, and beautiful china in her shop. 251-928-4657 or *tsm@silverandlace.com* for information.

Jessica Stalnaker of Empress Stationery designs beautiful suites of stationery for all occasions. Her work may be viewed at *www.empressstationery.com.*

Allison Banks of Allison R. Banks Designs makes her mark on the wedding and stationery world with her hand drawn monograms and invitations. *www.allisonrbanksdesigns.com*

Pandora de Balthazár has collected fine linens and offers these timeless creations with others. *www.pandoradebalthazar.com*

Amy Gray of Bobbins Design creates new wardrobes of linens for customers who want a fresh approach to entertaining. *www.bobbinsdesign.com*

Martha Lauren of Martha Lauren Linens has collected and sells vintage linens for her customers. *www.marthalauren7@gmail.com,* or 205-516-2633.

Sonia Showalter of Sonia Showalter Designs is the proprietor of her online embroidery design shop. *www.soniashowalterdesigns.com*

The Care and Keeping of Linen

Good linens can serve a lifetime and beyond if properly laundered and stored. Delicate fabrics and precious heirlooms are best surrendered to textile professionals, but most linens can be tended at home. Here are our suggestions for keeping cotton, linen, and cotton-linen-blend household treasures healthy.

ENJOY YOUR LINENS.
Frequent use extends the life of fabrics, so don't keep fine sheets and favorite table linens in reserve for fear that service will diminish their quality. Stashing linens in cupboards indefinitely allows fold lines to create stress on the fibers and promotes dry rot. Most textiles actually fare better when used and laundered regularly, so let them breathe, and appreciate their beauty.

TREAT STAINS PROMPTLY.
A gracious hostess need not fret when spills soil her table linens. Without a lapse in conversation, she can quickly dab the stain with a cold, wet cloth; rub a sprinkling of table salt over the spot; and cover the blemish with a napkin to avoid additional disturbance to the meal. After a dinner party, soak all table linens in an ice-water bath for a few hours or even overnight. Stains that do not come out in the bath can be further treated with a stain-removing formula before being laundered. Dishwashing liquid, lemon juice, vinegar, and mineral spirits are helpful stain remedies to keep on hand.

GO WITH THE GENTLE CYCLE.
For the most fragile fabrics, as well as table linens with delicate handwork or trim, hand washing in the sink with warm water and a mild detergent formulated for textiles is the safest option. Sturdier linens can withstand the tumble of a washing machine on the gentle cycle. Oxygenated bleach is safe for most textiles, but chlorine bleach is not recommended. Handle wet articles with care, squeezing out excess water without twisting or wringing the fabric. Allow vintage or fragile linens to air-dry.

TREAT YOUR BED.
Wash sheets weekly in warm water, turning patterned pillowcases inside out to keep colors vibrant. Freshly pressed sheets feel luxuriously new again, but many fabric blends are supple and inviting pulled straight from the dryer.

ADDRESS PRESSING ISSUES.
Crisp linens add polish to a home, but caution should be taken when ironing them. For best results, place a terry-cloth towel over the ironing board, and press damp linens with a dry iron. Delicate cloth should be sandwiched between the towel and a press cloth. If you are unsure how the fabric will handle heat, begin with the iron on the lowest setting, and test a small, inconspicuous area before increasing the heat. Keep a spray bottle of distilled water nearby, and spritz as needed to moisten the item. Iron embroidered linens on the wrong side to protect the needlework and to display the design to its best effect. Some textile experts do not recommend the use of starch—or they suggest starching only before use and laundering—as the carbohydrate can cause stored linens to yellow and attract insects.

GIVE LINENS A SOFT PLACE TO LAND.
Thoughtful planning yields storage options that prolong the life of treasured linens. Plastic bins do not allow air to circulate, so choose wire or painted wood shelving lined with acid-free paper or cotton fabric for best results. Rolling is gentler on fibers than folding, so consider wrapping a set of napkins or a collection of tea towels around a cardboard tube to avoid creases. A bundle of chalk tied with ribbon and hung in the linen closet draws moisture away from linens, while sprigs of lavender provide subtle fragrance.

A *Modern* SERVIETTE GUIDE

Ever-changing napkin sizes can leave hostesses confused about proper dimensions for table linens. Keep our convenient reference on hand when entertaining, and create a charming tablescape with confidence, no matter the occasion.

NAPKIN SIZES

"Large, snowy fields of linen that drape my lap and protect me, with a graciousness you can measure: That's what I'm looking for," laments well-traveled writer William J. Hamilton, who has noticed a shift in fine-restaurant accoutrements during the past twenty-five years from a generous 30-inch-square napkin to a more modest 22 inches. The contrast is even more pronounced when comparing napkins of Colonial Williamsburg, historically 36 inches square, to the standard 20-inch variety used at White House state dinners today. With household linens trending toward a smaller dinner napkin and a larger lunch napkin, Hamilton suggests that casual entertainers may opt for styles that can do double duty. Here is a contemporary guide for today's hostess to keep in mind:

- Formal dinner: 20 to 27 inches square
- Buffet: 18 to 27 inches square
- Informal dinner: 18 to 24 inches square
- Luncheon: 14 to 20 inches square
- Hors d'oeuvre: 13 inches square
- Tea: 12 inches square
- Folded cocktail: 6x9 inches
- Cocktail: 6 inches square

Resources

On Page 201 is the listing for Purveyors of Fine Linens and Embroidery

Companies that offer items shown in this book:
Biltmore Estate
www.biltmore.com
Replacements, Ltd.
www.replacements.com
Colonial Williamsburg
www.williamsburgmarketplace.com
Douglas Harris Jewelers
www.drharrisjewelers.com
Pottery Barn
www.potterybarn.com
Sasha Nicholas
www.sashanicholas.com
Sew Sheri Designs
www.sewsheri.com
Sur La Table
www.surlatable.com

The following companies are sources for machine embroidery monograms and designs:
Classic Sewing Magazine
www.classicsewingmagazine.com
Martha Pullen Company
www.marthapullen.com
Anna Bove Embroidery
www.annaboveembroidery.com
AriZona Embroidery Barn
www.azembroiderybarn.com
8 Claws and a Paw Embroidery
www.8clawsandapaw.com
Baby Lock Embroidery Machines and Fonts
www.babylock.com

Page 151, photography by Lieb Photographic, Michelle Lieb.

The exquisite christening gown on pages 156-157 is designed by **Connie Palmer** for *Classic Sewing Magazine* (*www.classicsewingmagazine.com*) with fabrics and lace from **Farmhouse Fabrics** (*www.farmhousefabrics.com*) and photographed by **Cynthia Pace Photography** (*www.cynthiapacephotography.com*).

Contributing Photographers of the wedding dresses:
Johnny Chauvin Photography
www.chauvinphotography.com
Phillip DuPree Photography
205-567-4104

Many of the features in this book are from *Victoria Magazine, Southern Lady Magazine* and *The Cottage Journal* all from Hoffman Media, LLC
www.hoffmanmedia.com